Tales From the Turf

Also by Steve Smith Eccles with Alan Lee

Turf Account

TALES FROM THE TURF

STEVE SMITH ECCLES
with Alan Lee

PARTRIDGE PRESS

LONDON · NEW YORK · TORONTO · SYDNEY · AUCKLAND

TRANSWORLD PUBLISHERS LTD
61–63 Uxbridge Road, London W5 5SA

TRANSWORLD PUBLISHERS (AUSTRALIA) PTY LTD
15–23 Helles Avenue, Moorebank, NSW 2170

TRANSWORLD PUBLISHERS (NZ) LTD
Cnr Moselle and Waipareira Aves,
Henderson, Auckland

Published 1988 by Partridge Press
a division of Transworld Publishers Ltd
Copyright © Steve Smith Eccles and Alan Lee 1988
Illustrations © Graham Thompson

British Library Cataloguing in Publication Data

Smith Eccles, Steve
  Tales from turf.
  1. Great Britain. National Hunt racing
  I. Title II. Lee, Alan, 1954–
  798.4'5'0941

  ISBN 1-85225-071-2

Printed and bound in Great Britain by
Mackays of Chatham PLC, Chatham, Kent

Contents

Introduction

For ten months of each year, six days a week and in every corner of England, I make my living by riding horses over obstacles. It is a hectic, demanding existence. Sometimes, it is a dangerous one too. There are moments of euphoria, but these are treats to savour in a business which can injure the soul as much as the body, a business which is a public entertainment but a private examination of character for all those involved.

Don't get me wrong. I am not complaining. Life has been good to me and, whenever I find my enthusiasm low, my motivation lacking, I remind myself what else I might be doing instead. It does not take long. I come from coalmining stock in Derbyshire. My fancy name might fool a lot of people but the truth is I could very easily have followed the family tradition and gone down the pit. I need only to reflect on that to know that I am exceedingly fortunate to be doing a job I thoroughly enjoy, and one which gives me enormous satisfaction most of the time.

All of us, however, whether we work in an office, down the pit or out in the open, need the occasional diversion from the serious side of employment. We need a release. My escape comes in humour. I have always loved laughing and, with expert coaching from the likes of John Francome, I have developed a keen sense of the ridiculous. I love to laugh with others, and I admit I am not averse to playing the occasional practical joke, providing the recipient takes it in the spirit intended.

To laugh, often at oneself, is a great release from tension – and there is plenty of that in horseracing. After ten years at, or very near, the top of my profession, I endured the worst season of my career in 1987–8. It was as if the fates had ganged up to concoct a colourful but constant nightmare. Everything that could have gone wrong did go wrong – some things more than once. I had innumerable falls, once breaking my arm, suffered silently while my retaining stable virtually shut down with a virus and then, when the season was reaching its climax, saw several of my classiest rides ruled out by serious injury.

If there was ever a season to finish a jockey, this was it, but, while I do not deny I occasionally felt depressed, sometimes retiring to my private 'snug' at home for a lengthy spell of self-appraisal, I came through it smiling. I managed that because, unlike far too many of the riders I see in racing these days, I refuse to get to the point where I can see nothing outside my job.

Racing is a way of life; of course it is. But to many jockeys (and trainers, come to that) it is a dangerous obsession, a solemn daily routine to be negotiated rather than a sport to be enjoyed. I am not suggesting that anyone should be casual or careless; there is too much at stake for that. But does it hurt to laugh occasionally? I think not. In fact, my view is that a lot of the new generation of jockeys will self-destruct, as personalities, because they have no sense of humour, no life outside the saddle. They take themselves far too seriously.

By nature, I suppose I am an adventurer and a fighter, though not in the nasty sense of the word. I honestly don't believe there is any malice in me, and I will take a big detour to avoid any potential hassle. If, however, I am cornered or compromised, I am at my most dangerous, because I will come out fighting. This characteristic may well show itself in my style and pattern of riding; I don't imagine it would do for every critic, but it has served me well this past decade and, although I may be nearing the end of the road, there are one or two more winners I wish to ride before hanging up my boots. Most of all, I think I am reluctant to sacrifice the lifestyle I have earned for myself, the routine I have grown to love and, very decidedly, the enjoyment which comes with it.

I hope, in the pages of this book, that I can transmit some of that enjoyment, some of the ridiculous, hilarious, funny and sad incidents which have followed me through life; I hope also that my recollections of what has befallen friends and colleagues in the racing game will cause amusement. I hope no one takes offence, because it is not meant to be that type of book. It is a celebration of something I hold very dear – the fact that there is fun to be had within the most serious of vocations.

Travelling Time

I often think that it is not so much the riding which is hard work in a jockey's life – it is the miles he has to cover before even getting on the horse. Most of the busier National Hunt jockeys drive upwards of 50,000 miles each season, often in the worst conditions winter has to offer. Many is the time, driving home utterly exhausted on a dark, wet and murky December night, that I have longed for the days when jockeys did most of their travelling by train. The motorways changed all that, and, apart from the very occasional hop in a helicopter (an annual treat for some of us, but a regular way of life for the jet–setting flat jockeys), all of our travel is now done on the roads.

I am luckier than some in that I like cars and enjoy driving. In recent years, I have usually owned a Porsche, which is not only very comfortable but fast enough to take some of the pain out of the long and tedious hours on the motorways. I play music loudly – a diversity of tastes – and I also have a car telephone, a facility now owned by an ever-increasing number of jockeys and trainers because it allows us to be available to take and book rides even when we are not at home.

No matter how great one's affection for motoring, however, I contend it is impossible to enjoy every one of the 200-plus journeys which must be made during a jumping season. Some are plain insufferable. I have often arrived home with my eyes feeling as heavy as lead, thanking God that I managed to keep them open and be relatively alert after endless miles in driving rain – all at the end of a day's work!

I have had my share of minor accidents and my share of scrapes with the police. Some of my more memorable driving debacles, however, have been largely self-induced. . .

One February afternoon at Ascot, I dismounted from my only ride of the meeting just after 2 p.m. I got home precisely twenty-three hours later.

The trouble began when I met up with Peter Shilton, the England goalkeeper. Peter is a great racing fan and an old friend. One drink led to another and, as the following day's racing had already been abandoned due to frost, we agreed to head up to the West End for a night out. Sensibly, or so I thought, I left my car at Ascot.

By the time I emerged from our chosen nightspot at about 3 a.m. it was snowing heavily. I hailed a taxi and persuaded the driver, against his better judgement, to brave the worsening conditions and get me back to the racecourse. Then, already cursing myself for having set out on this adventure, I pointed the car towards Newmarket.

Three hours later I had got as far as Royston, and I could take no more. Totally exhausted by peering through the driving snow, I pulled off the road and settled back in the hope that things might improve. I slept for two hours, but at 9 a.m. the sight which greeted me was even more alarming. Not only had the snow not relented, it had, if anything, become worse. Half of the car was now submerged; I had to force the door open to confirm my worst fears. I was hopelessly stuck.

There was nothing for it but to seek help on foot. I waded across a field towards the first house I could pick out through the still raging blizzard. It turned out to be a farmhouse and, after a good deal of grovelling and genuflecting, I succeeded in convincing the farmer that his tractor was my only hope of escape. He grudgingly emerged from the warm, towed me out and I continued on my way.

It really is not that far from Royston to Newmarket but it took me another two hours. I pulled into the drive of my cottage, shattered beyond words, nine hours after setting off from Ascot. Next time I agree to a night out in the West End, I promised myself as I crawled into bed, I will check the weather forecast first!

Back in the days when Ian Watkinson and I used to go racing together almost every day, we organised a bizarre competition. Driving on alternate days, we would each try to gather as many points as possible during the journey. Points were awarded for the reactions of fellow motorists, on a sliding scale which read: 5 points for a shaken fist; 10 points for a V-sign; 15 points for flashing lights, shaken fist and V-sign from the same driver, and so on.

Both of us put up some outrageous displays in our time but Ian beat the all–comers' record by scoring more than 100 points on a single journey between Newmarket and Cheltenham. I swear that if he had met himself coming back the other way, he would be dead.

Jockeys are generally running to a tight schedule. By the time they have ridden out in the morning, changed and set off for the races, there is little margin for such things as traffic jams. Sometimes, drastic action is called for. Holiday times are the worst and, a couple of seasons back, I found myself stranded in hopeless queues twice in a fortnight. Knowing that simply to sit and suffer would mean missing my booked rides, I took to the hard shoulder of the motorway and just put my foot down and hoped. The first time, I got away with it; the second, all I got was a booking from a vigilant policeman who was utterly unimpressed by my excuses.

I have never dared, however, to copy one jockey friend of mine who, on being stopped for exceeding 100 m.p.h. on a motorway and told he would be sure to lose his licence, gloomily informed the policeman that it was of no concern to him because he was suffering from a killer disease and had only a few months left to live. It must have been an Oscar-winning performance because the officer, shamed into pity, put away his notebook, patted my pal on the back and sent him on his way.

Sally Oliver, the Midlands trainer responsible for that good hurdler, Aonoch, among others, once had to make an embarrassing admission. One of her horses had won at Bangor-on-Dee, the very remote Shropshire course, in circumstances which persuaded the stewards to hold an inquiry. They went through the usual procedure of making a public address announcement, calling for Mrs Oliver, but she was nowhere to be found. It transpired that she had never been to Bangor before and, on consulting her map, had made her way to the other town of the same name about 100 miles away on the North Wales coast!

We do not often get to fly anywhere during the racing season, but the occasional foreign trip makes a pleasant diversion. I remember going to Belgium with a very distinguished British team, made up of John Francome, Jonjo O'Neill, Peter Scudamore and myself. The flight across was uneventful, we won the match against the Belgians and then, it must be confessed, we indulged pretty liberally in the hospitality on offer. As a result, there were some grey faces at the airport the following morning, and grey rapidly turned to green when our chartered light aircraft began to bounce across the Channel in gusting winds. Only 'Franc' was completely unaffected – and insufferably cheerful about the whole thing. Seeing that 'Scu' was feeling particularly rough, John handed him a sick bag. When we landed, he took back the used bag and paraded through the airport with it, announcing the famous sportsman who had provided it. 'Scu', whose face had gone through the grey and green stage, was by then a brighter shade of red.

Trains are almost a redundant mode of travel among jockeys and trainers, but there are exceptions to every rule. . .

A couple of years ago, Rod Simpson, the flamboyant Lambourn trainer, decided to send two horses to a flat meeting at Carlisle. Now, it is a very long way from Berkshire to Cumbria, and the transportation of the horses is a hefty expense, so Rod was plainly confident that there were some easy pickings to be had. His regular jockey, Simon Whitworth, was engaged elsewhere, so Rod offered the two rides to his Lambourn neighbour Billy Newnes and suggested that, rather than attempt a twelve-hour round trip by road, they should take the train. This, apparently, proved more complicated than Rod had suspected, as there are surprisingly few trains running direct from London to Carlisle.

Undaunted, he made the bookings for the upward journey and, when they arrived at Carlisle station, Rod checked with the ticket-desk for the times of trains returning to London. It turned out that the last train back left Carlisle at 4.35 p.m. This was ideal for Rod, whose last runner was at 3.30, but not so clever for Billy, who had taken a spare ride in the 4.30 race. Not wanting to alarm his jockey unnecessarily, Rod kept this piece of information to himself.

The day was going well. Both the Simpson horses had won, Rod had enjoyed a nice touch by backing them as a double, and the course management had presented him with a magnum of champagne to recognise his first runners, and first winners, at Carlisle. Amid the joy in the winner's enclosure, however, Rod slipped the bad news about the train to Billy, who predictably panicked.

Rodney Simpson, however, is a man of considerable resources, and having placated Billy and assured him that all would be well, he gave him his instructions. He was to jump straight off his final ride, have a taxi waiting, and get to the station as soon after 4.30 as possible. Rod promised to hold up the train until he got there, though in saying this with great confidence he admitted to himself that he had no idea how to accomplish it.

Leaving Billy, a little agitated, at the course, Rod set off to the station and awaited the train. It came in at 4.25, whereupon Rod, a plan now taking shape, left his bags on the platform and walked out of the station and a hundred yards down the street to a supermarket. He collected a trolley, circled the store, bought and paid for a bag of crisps and then wheeled his trolley back down the road, into the station and right on to the platform where the train was still waiting. It was now 4.33 p.m.

Enjoying himself hugely, he loaded his bags on to the trolley, stepped into the carriage and pulled the trolley after him. It stuck in the doorway, just as he had known it would, but Rod kept pulling until the bars bent under the strain. Then, satisfied with his handiwork, he sat down and waited for someone to notice that a trolley was wedged half in and half out of a carriage door.

At 4.39 p.m. a breathless and anxious Billy Newnes sprinted onto the platform and leaped aboard the train. It was another eleven minutes before the trolley could be released, Rod all the time offering innocent apologies to the station staff and loudly wondering how he could have been so stupid.

Just to complete the coup, Rod then took Billy up into a first-class compartment, where they sat, illicitly, happily supping the hard-earned champagne, an eventful day successfully concluded.

Weighing-Room

The weighing-room is the jockeys' sanctuary, the place where temper can be released, tantrums enacted or triumphs relived, in absolute privacy. Officially, no one other than the course officials is permitted in the weighing-room until racing is over; even trainers are not supposed to venture through the door, which, considering some of the conversation topics, is probably just as well. It is a place of business, a hectic and sometimes hot-headed area, where riders, often cramped, frequently wet and sometimes aching, prepare between rides, discussing what is to come and what has gone before.

To suggest it has the solemn atmosphere of a City office, however, would be deceitful. On every day, at every meeting, there is humour in the weighing-room. Occasionally it may be racing's black humour, a laugh at the expense of someone else in the game, but there is sufficient camaraderie and concern within our ranks to ensure it never becomes malicious. Much more often, the humour comes from a prank or a funny story, and in racing, as in the rest of life, the fun and the frequency of this depend on who you happen to be with at the time.

During my years as a jockey, two men in particular have landed me in more scrapes, yet given me many more laughs, than all the rest of the profession put together. Ian Watkinson, not for nothing known as the 'Iron Man', was the first to lead me astray; the great John Francome was the second. I make no apologies for the fact that their names occur with some frequency during this book. Their personalities attracted, maybe actively invited, humour, and things certainly seemed to happen when they were around. The weighing-room, for all my own efforts to enliven it, has seemed a duller, more mundane place since they both retired. Some of what follows here may help to explain what I mean.

Mention the bell at Newbury to jockeys who have been around for a few years, and you are guaranteed to raise a laugh. The first part of the story is amusing enough, the sequel still perplexes certain stewards to this day. Let me explain. . .

Most courses have a bell rigged up in the weighing-room. It is rung by one of the attendants, about seven minutes before the scheduled 'off' of each race, and is the signal for jockeys to file out to the parade ring for the ritual meeting with connections. On the day in question, Newbury had just fitted a new bell which had an indecent, clanging ring, so loud that John Francome spilled his tea when it went off prior to the first race.

We put up with this for two races before 'Franc' took action. Using a pair of women's tights (jockeys, unbeknown to many, often wear them under their breeches) he tied what amounted to a silencer on the bell. His intention had been to muffle the noise, but his efforts were actually so successful that no sound was emitted whatever when the attendant pressed his button. We were contentedly idling around, chatting and joking in the usual fashion, when one of the stewards, plainly irate, rushed in and demanded to know what was going on, as the jockeys for the next race should have been mounted in the parade ring five minutes earlier.

The race concerned was, I think, a handicap chase with only six or seven runners; inevitably, it was late away, and, when we returned to weigh in, the stewards summoned all the jockeys involved to an inquiry.

We had a rapid conference before going in and elected Bill Smith as our spokesman. Bill is a natural talker, as is evidenced by his subsequent career as a television summariser, and he launched eloquently into a complex explanation of why the delay could in no way be blamed upon the innocent riders. Francome was positioned directly behind Bill, who was standing, much like a naughty schoolboy in the headmaster's study, with his hands behind his back.

Out of sight of the stewards, 'Franc' unzipped his flies and slipped his penis into Bill's hands. The expression on Bill's face changed rapidly from innocence, to puzzlement, to utter horror as he realised what had happened. He leaped like a scalded cat, the rest of us burst into fits of laughter and 'Franc', who had rapidly replaced the offending instrument and zipped up, stood looking like a choirboy. The stewards plainly assumed we had all taken leave of our senses, and the inquiry broke up amid a good deal of irritation and bewilderment.

Kempton Park is a popular venue among jockeys since the building of a new weighing-room with the best amenities of any in the country. The food and drink service is worth the trip alone, and there is even a pool table to amuse us before and during racing. With the new weighing-room, however, came a new doorman who was not quite such good news. He was the type who was always cadging from the jockeys – cigarettes, sweets, fruit; whatever was going, he would be there. His greed began to annoy us, and one day it got the better of him.

John Francome and I were in the loo, standing at adjacent urinals; John was staring at the floor when he suddenly exclaimed. He vanished from the room and reappeared within seconds brandishing a sweet bag with some lemon drops in it. For the life of me I could not imagine what he was up to, until he pointed mischievously at the base of the urinals, which contained a batch of yellow disinfectant squares. At a glance they did not look unlike the lemon cubes in

John's sweet bag and suddenly I realised what had occurred to him.

Keeping one of the real sweets back, he scooped up the disinfectant cubes into the bag. He then carefully put the remaining lemon drop on top, and as we marched back into the weighing-room he made a great play of offering me a sweet. I took the real one and, no sooner had I put it in my mouth than the doorman had taken the bait. He was over in a flash, helping himself from the bag, and, without bothering to examine what he had got, he popped a 'sweet' into his mouth.

It was five, long seconds before he realised something was wrong. He made an explosive choking sound and rushed out of the room. We spent the rest of the afternoon watching him spitting and making thoroughly unpleasant faces . . . a cruel trick maybe – but he never bothered us for anything again.

The first time I rode at the Cheltenham Festival I was just out of apprenticeship, very young and very naive. Ian Watkinson had initially become a friend because we both came from Newmarket and, seeing an impressionable kid with whom some fun could be had, he suggested a prank from which I was lucky to escape intact.

As I had no weight problems in those days, I was filling in the hour before racing happily chomping through a giant hot dog, with a mountain of fried onions on top, and swilling a can of Coke. The smell, I now realise, must have been unbearable to anyone wasting to make a light weight. At the time, however, it never occurred to me, and when Ian suggested I should walk into the sauna and show my hot dog around I agreed without a second thought.

I blundered into a sweating, suffering group which included Bob Champion and Philip Blacker, amongst others. I was in the sauna no more than three seconds, but that was quite long enough to see the murderous expressions on their faces.

I have never moved so fast in my life and, for the rest of that day, I was careful to keep out of the way of everyone who had been in the sauna. It is not a trick I shall be trying again, and I can imagine my own reaction, heavier as I am these days, if anyone tried it on me.

*　　*　　*

In the years when Ian Watkinson and I travelled together a good deal, we had a regular routine on the eve of the Cheltenham Festival. We had discovered a very well stocked joke shop in the town, and at the expenditure of no more than a few pounds each we could be guaranteed some fun during the week.

One year, we bought a supply of sweets which had a hot mustard filling. We caught any number of people with these, producing a reaction not too dissimilar to that of the Kempton doorman on chewing into a disinfectant drop. By the final day of the meeting we were running out of targets . . . but there is always an Irishman to fool!

We gave Paddy Broderick one of the rogue sweets and, along with the rest of the jockeys – most of whom were by now in the know – awaited the usual reaction. Now Paddy was a good enough jockey to have won the Champion Hurdle, among many other big events, but his mind often seemed to be stuck in neutral. This was a case in point. He chewed through the sweet and swallowed it, mustard and all, without a word or a change of expression. If we were shocked by this, there was more to come. After riding in the next race, Paddy came up and asked us for another, adding utterly seriously: 'They are bloody good cough sweets, boys.'

A different batch of sweets, from the same source, looked equally appealing and had an even more distasteful filling. If you chewed through these, you discovered something which tasted very rubbery – which it was. The filling was a condom.

These caused great hilarity, but I thought we might be chancing our luck a little when we gave one to the distinguished Jockey Club starter, Sir John Guise. To my great relief, Sir John not only appreciated the joke but, being a good partygoer, set off to the shop in question to buy some for himself!

Another lavatorial story involving John Francome and myself involved the clerk of scales at Newbury, who used to be a chap named Major Manning and, for obvious reasons, became known to us all – except, of course, to his face – as 'Bernard'. If he was not very popular among the jockeys, this was generally because he did his job rather too meticulously for our liking. The clerk of scales wields a good deal of power over our lives, and frustrations are inevitable if, after a hectic round of wasting, you are adjudged a pound overweight for the sake of no more than a few ounces. Owners and trainers are quite naturally reluctant to put up overweight on their horses, and Major Manning at his most dictatorial could sometimes sour relations with connections for an entire afternoon.

On the day in question he had been handing out extra pounds with considerable relish and was the subject of a concerted weighing-room moan. John Francome and myself, for some strange reason, appeared to be his particular targets for the meeting and, as such, we were in bad odour with our trainers and in a thoroughly bad mood with 'Bernard'.

The chance to extract revenge arose out of nothing and, I have to say, again involved the use of a private part of the anatomy. During a break between rides, 'Franc' and I were in the jockeys' tearoom, bemoaning our lot, sipping half a cup of tea and enviously eyeing the sandwiches, a mere bite of which would have given 'Bernard' another ounce to crow about.

Quite by coincidence, one of the doormen came through and asked the tea lady for a cup of tea for Major Manning. It was duly dispensed and, just as the doorman was about to make off with it, 'Franc' stopped him, took it out of his hands and told him we would give it to the Major. For a moment I thought he had gone a little soft in the head after the trials of the afternoon and was trying to woo 'Bernard' in a different way. I then caught sight of the glint in his eyes and knew I had misjudged him.

He tested the tea with his finger and, finding it was the usual luke-warm common to so many racecourses, unzipped his breeches (again!), pulled out his cock and dipped it into the tea. After a few moments of uncontrollable laughter I did the same thing and then, angelically straightfaced, we duly carried the cup through, recalled the doorman and, to his complete bewilderment, got him to complete the delivery.

A few moments later we sidled out into the scales area and leant on

SLURP!

the railing, from where we watched the Major thirstily drain every drop of his thoroughly impure tea. Now and again he looked across curiously at the smirks covering our faces; I don't think he ever found out the reason for them.

The snappiest dresser among the current generation of jockeys is probably Graham Bradley. I go back a little farther than most, however, and when I began riding the peacock of the weighing-room was undoubtedly Martin Blackshaw. He dressed for racing much more smartly than many would dress for dinner at a high-class restaurant and, as usual with this type, he was immensely proud of his clothes.

One day, he came racing in a three-piece white suit, with which he was evidently very pleased. He accepted the customary wolf-whistles of colleagues with good grace. He did not accept what happened next at all. The incorrigible Ian Watkinson had with him a pot of disappearing ink, purchased from the infamous Cheltenham joke shop. 'Watty' knew it was disappearing ink, Martin did not, so when a generous measure of it was thrown over his brand new suit the reaction was instant and ferocious. 'Watty', hard man that he is, had to run for it, so violent was the look on Martin's face. He took a great deal of persuading, from a group of us splitting our sides with mirth, that the ink would indeed vanish, and it is fair to say he was not in the best of moods for the rest of the day.

Cheating The Scales

Most jockeys have spent some of their most uncomfortable hours in the sauna and some of their most uncomfortable minutes on the scales. I may be luckier than the majority, as for the great part of my career I have had very few weight worries, but it catches up with us all eventually, and in the last couple of seasons I have needed to pay far more attention to what and when I eat, always with that dreaded moment in mind when I will sit on the scales and hear the awful word 'overweight' uttered by the official-looking gent in front of me.

I suppose it can't be very much fun being a clerk of the scales, knowing that however nice a chap you may be, most jockeys consider you their public enemy number one, while more than a few are trying to pull the wool over your eyes. Perhaps on the whole it is easiest to be the vindictive type! Similarly, it is certainly no fun being a heavy jockey, perennially obliged to take whatever steps are available, or within the scope of clever invention, in order to save a few pounds and avert the reproachful words of trainers and owners!

For those who don't like saunas, or find them of limited help, various other drastic slimming aids are available. One of the most widely used is the tablet known in the jockeys' vernacular as the 'pee-pill'. It does exactly what you would expect from its name and the loss of fluid from the body can sometimes make the difference on a day when desperate measures are demanded in order to make a weight. Timing, however, is of the essence – and I wish I had known that when I turned to the 'pee-pill' as a last resort.

It was a winter day a few years ago. The meeting was at Fontwell, and I had been asked to ride at around my minimum weight. As I had not ridden at all for several days, and was in the middle of a pretty bleak spell all round, I was anxious to take the ride, so, a few hours before racing, I swallowed one of the pills and waited for it to take effect.

When I was changing into my riding gear, I was still waiting, and I mentioned as much to a mate in the weighing-room. He laughed and told me I ought to have taken the pill at breakfast time because it needed several hours to take effect. This was not good news, but there was absolutely nothing I could do to reverse the process. Much as I had begun to fear, I was on the way to post for my first ride of the day, a novice-chase, when the urge overtook me. Within seconds, I was frantic to relieve myself and I knew there was no possibility of hanging on until the race was over.

I took the only way out. The runners were all circling at the start and, as there was a maximum field, I reasoned it would take some while for the starter to check all the girths prior to getting us under way. I jumped off my horse, handed the reins to one of the starter's assistants with a semi-audible explanation, and sprinted down to the first fence, where, with a sigh of satisfaction, I set about losing a few ounces. I then discovered the other thing no one had told me about this bloody pill – it makes you desperate to pee, but it can take a long time to happen! Not to put too fine a point on it, I stood there with my breeches round my ankles for about five minutes, growing steadily more agitated, before at long last the action started.

The upshot of all this was that the race went off three minutes late and there were some embarrassing questions to answer. The postscript, which I discovered only some time later, is that the race was being covered live by SIS who, bored by the delayed start, turned one of their cameras on the hapless figure standing at the first fence. My peeing problems were, apparently, beamed live into the nation's betting shops. I understand the film, showing me hastily dismounting and scampering off down the course, is now in the hands of BBC TV's 'Question of Sport' team, and it is a certainty to crop up in the 'What Happened Next?' slot.

Ian Watkinson's build was ideally too big for a jockey. His weight problems were constant and enormous. In the summer months he would blow up to something over 12 stone, probably much more his natural weight, yet during the season he would still somehow ride at the minimum 10 stone. He reckoned he had two sets of clothes – one size for the winter and another for the summer.

He took every available pill to keep his weight down and, during the early weeks of each season, he would habitually drive to racing meetings wearing a sweat-suit, zipped up tight to the collar and with elastic bands round his ankles to prevent the sweat escaping. He would wind up all the windows and turn the heater on full. This, I must remind you, is in August, traditionally the hottest month of the British summer, and while he may possibly have felt the benefit of the torture, one S. Smith Eccles, his regular passenger, certainly did not. I used to sit next to him dressed in nothing but my underpants, my face as red as a lobster. I honestly cannot imagine what pedestrians must have thought as they peered at the exceedingly odd couple in this car. . .!

One of the most common means of 'cheating' the scales is to weigh out with an absurdly light saddle. I don't know that it goes on so much these days, but some of the characters of old would apparently do this on a regular basis, discreetly swapping the 'miniature' for a more reasonable saddle after passing the scales at the correct weight. I'm told that Barry Brogan, the highly controversial jockey of the 1960s and 70s, had a cheating saddle which proved very popular one day at Newcastle – no fewer than five jockeys weighed out with it!

The system was simple. Brogan went first, passed the scales, walked to the door of the weighing-room, handed the saddle to an accomplice and returned. The accomplice then strolled round to the back of the building, passed the saddle through a convenient window to the next jockey, and so the routine was repeated. I imagine it became quite a challenge.

John Francome was a connoisseur of cheating. He elevated it to an art form and very often needed to, for his natural riding weight was far heavier than the average. 'Franc' was brazen about it – not for him the 'cheating saddle' – sometimes he would not bother with a saddle at all. When he went to sit on the scales he had an elastic band around his thigh, through which he looped his breastgirth and a polystyrene pad, arranged to make it look as if he were concealing an ordinary saddle. I'm pretty sure I would never have carried it off successfully, but John got away with it time after time.

I used to believe I could ride on the flat with Francome around to help. Although I had relatively few problems, there was the odd occasion when I knew I was a couple of pounds heavier than I ought to be. John, wearing his most innocent expression, would accompany me to the scales and, with timing the essence, stick his toe under the machine just as I sat on it. By careful manoeuvring, he then tipped the scales back to the correct weight.

He once asked me to return the favour but I managed to make a complete hash of what had always appeared a perfectly simple operation. John needed to pass at 10 stone 7 pounds and, although I got my toe under the scales successfully enough, I could not keep the needle steady. It bobbed up and down between 10 and 11 stone until, inevitably, the clerk of the scales smelt a rat. We managed to pass it off as a joke, but it was a nasty moment.

Ian Watkinson liked going to Bangor for one particular reason. Apparently, it used to be the only course in the country where the base of the scales chair was level with the surrounding floor. To an experienced campaigner like 'Watty', this reduced the business of cheating to child's play. He would wear the lightest of boots, which were really no more than leather socks, and curl a toe off the edge of the scales on to the floor. By applying pressure through the toe, he reckoned he could take off any poundage he required.

The 'cheating boots' became an established part of the Watkinson repertoire. They were, if you like, among his most useful props. A particularly vigilant clerk of the scales named Hopkins, however, recognised the ruse and determined to make life difficult. At Stratford one day, Watty sat on the scales wearing these flimsy shoes and Mr Hopkins innocently asked him if he meant to ride in them. This, of course, was the last thing on Ian's mind – he intended to change them for something more sturdy as soon as he was back in the weighing-room – but Mr Hopkins was a step ahead of him. He asked Ian to put his feet up on the desk and then, very carefully and deliberately, he autographed each boot and informed the crestfallen Watkinson that he would check them when the race was over. 'I had no option. I had to wear them,' Ian recalls. 'I put racecards inside the soles to try and ease the pressure but they still almost cut my feet off. Just to make the point, though, I weighed out still wearing them later in the afternoon, when I had 12 stone 7 pounds in a handicap chase and didn't need them at all!'

Mr Hopkins, who plainly had something of a love–hate relationship with Watty, also caught him out one day at Southwell. Ian was perhaps a little blasé about his 'cheating' by this stage and it cost him dearly. He had promised to do 10–3 on a chaser for a rather cantankerous Midlands trainer. He wore the cheating boots, sat on the scales and manipulated the needle to 10–3, but something then distracted him at the crucial moment. Mr Hopkins, who evidently knew very well what was going on, smugly instructed him to go back to the weighing-room for four pounds of lead. Ian, scarcely able to believe his ears, glanced up and saw to his horror that he had been pushing too hard on the floor – the needle had dropped to 9–13.

One of Watty's most ambitiously risky cheating performances was on a chaser called Hopeful Hill. It is a story best told by the man himself:

'I had won a seller on Hopeful Hill when he was trained by Earl Jones. After the race, he was bought by a trainer named Barton, who did not ask me to ride him again. I was slightly peeved, but no more than that, because he was a big, ignorant horse, built like a giraffe and with a mind all of his own. The following season he had run four or five times, each with a different jockey and each time refusing to set off. By this time he was not only in danger of exhausting everyone's patience but of being warned off by the Jockey Club. He was in at Wolverhampton one day and I was there to ride in another race. Mr Barton, who I still hardly knew, approached me at the races and asked me if I would ride him. He told me he had 10–2 and bridled when I said I would do 10–7. When I pointed out that he seemed most unlikely to start the race anyway, he mumbled something and agreed I could ride him at that weight.

'He added that if he was ridden properly he would win. This rather put my back up, so I cheated like hell to get through at 10–7. I needed the cheating boots and a one-pound saddle, and by the time I had swapped both for heavier items, I suspect I was about 11–2 when I went out to ride. I kept consoling myself with the thought that he wouldn't set off anyway, so I would not have to weigh in – I knew very well that I stood to get a three-month suspension if I was caught.

'The trainer told me to keep trotting the horse around on his toes at the start. Not being very anxious for him to take any part, I did the opposite and allowed him to stand mulishly still. To my utter surprise and alarm, though, he took off like a rocket as soon as the tapes went up and he jumped the first in front. I spent most of the race trying to pull him out of contention but, fortunately, some of the others were too good for him anyway. He was lying about fifth when we jumped the last and I pulled him up on the run-in, walked him past the line and looked anxiously down at his legs to give anyone watching me the impression that I feared he had gone lame. This little performance was just a precaution – once a day, not just the placed jockeys but every rider in the race has to weigh-in if he has completed the course. Those who fall or pull-up are exempt. I was able to walk rapidly past the scales, shout 'pulled up' to the clerk and make the safety of the weighing-room.

'The clerk happened to be my old friend Mr Hopkins and he was also on duty at the next day's meeting at Nottingham. I was walking through the car park on my way into the races when he hailed me from his car. He was reading a copy of *Sporting Life* and he pointed accusingly at the summary of the previous day's meeting. "That horse you rode in the chase," he said, "You told me you pulled up, but it's got you down here as finishing fifth." I put on my most innocent expression, took a deep breath and replied: "I shouldn't worry about that, sir, they give those press jobs to anyone these days." '

Roy Mangan was another jockey who had to devote as much thought to wasting and cheating as he did to finding rides. He had some crazy ideas about how to lose weight, notably by wearing a helium-filled vest, and he claimed he could cheat two or three pounds by stringing the ties of his cap through his whip and resting the stick on the floor.

He was caught out once when finishing third and being obliged to weigh in. The clerk of the scales dryly announced that he was seven pounds more than he ought to have been but then, to Roy's surprise, waved him on without another word. Back in the weighing-room, Roy was ready to celebrate this remarkable escape when he felt a hand on his shoulder. He turned to find himself confronted by the clerk. 'I don't know what you did before that race, Roy,' he said, 'but don't ever try it on me again.' Roy tells me that his respect and appreciation for the man were so great that he obeyed him to the letter.

Back in the 1960s, a major, well-known even now in racing circles, used to ride his own horses in hunter chases. Being a big man he had to waste painfully even to manage 12 stone (the weight at which most hunter races are run) but he had discovered in the course of life that his military rank earned him a good deal of respect.

One day, having failed to make his required weight by conventional wasting, he sat on the scales quite blatantly without a saddle. All he had was a sponge over his arm, one leather and an iron looped through his finger. He called out his name and nominated weight and fixed the young, impressionable clerk of the scales with his most icily superior stare.

Shrinking back into his seat, the clerk gazed at the man who so obviously had no saddle and simply replied: 'Yes, sir, Major, sir, that's fine, thank you.'

Behind The Scenes

Jump jockeys are a generally contented breed. We tend to get on pretty well together, united by the common ground of risk and danger as much as anything else. There are times, however, when tempers will flare and the customarily friendly environment of the weighing-room becomes a temporary battle-ground. Most days of the week, you can expect at least one decent weighing-room ruck, usually emanating from a spot of rough riding and two different versions of who was to blame. Sometimes, the upsets occur when senior jockeys sound off at some of their younger and more reckless colleagues; sometimes, anger comes in the form of a monologue – a jockey giving vent to his feelings over something an owner or trainer has said to him. Usually, whatever the strength of feeling, the scene is quickly forgotten. Grudges do not sit happily within a claustrophobic community such as ours.

The parade ring is another area where much is said, frustratingly out of earshot of the racegoer who would give a great deal to know what passes between the connections of his particular fancy. On most occasions, he would be dismayed by the banality of the conversation – a time-filling exercise prior to mounting, all serious instructions having been conveyed at an earlier hour – but, just occasionally, he would be intrigued, amused or even shocked!

I have only once come to blows with another jockey. I'm not proud of it, and I sincerely hope it never happens again. Looking back on it, however, it must have made for a very spectacular scene.

It all took place at Stratford, the small but extremely well-patronised Midlands track, as popular with trainers as it is with the punters. If jockeys have any complaints about the course they normally concern the fact that it is among the tightest in the country – you are on the turn for most of the circuit, and this can sometimes lead to some unseemly scrimmaging. This was the case in the incident concerned, which happened a good few years ago and involved myself and Craig Smith, something of a specialist around the Midlands tracks.

Craig was in front, and I was tracking him on a decent horse called Sundance Kid. Going into the last bend before the home straight, Craig's horse, tiring, drifted off the rails just enough for me to seize the chance to go through on the inner. Sensing, rather than seeing my manoeuvre, Craig deliberately steered his horse back across my path. The tussle went on right round the turn and into the straight, accompanied by a good deal of shouting and swearing from both of us.

My horse had a little in hand and, once we had crossed the last flight, I was able to beat Craig's for speed and win the race. The row, however, had only just begun. A few more words were snarled between us as we walked the horses back to the winners' enclosure and hostilities resumed in earnest in the weighing-room.

It was one of those racing incidents where neither party will admit any responsibility. I thought he was in the wrong, he thought it was all my fault. After a good deal of acrimonious dialogue, I decided it had gone on long enough. I told him to forget it, to shut up – or I would whack him. It was not, at the time, said with any purpose, but it failed to stop him anyway. He was walking away from me, towards the swing doors which lead out of the weighing-room into the annexe occupied by the clerk of the scales, when he turned and called me a particularly unpleasant name.

Something snapped. I rushed over, tapped him on the shoulder and, as he turned to face me, caught him square on the jaw with an uppercut of such perfection that it would have done me credit in any boxing ring.

Craig reeled backwards and burst through the swing doors, landing with a thud beside the clerk of the scales' desk. From the other side of the doors it must have been like a scene from a cowboy film, some villain being smashed through the saloon doors into the dusty street. There were quite a lot of people in that area but, luckily for me, none of them were stewards. The incident was never reported to anyone in authority and Craig and I actually get on well these days. It may be my imagination, though, but I would swear he is rather civil to me during races!

Cartmel is one of British racing's delightful curiosities. It is a track tucked away within the Lake District, catering purely for holiday racing and attracting quite phenomenal crowds. It has an atmosphere all of its own – both for spectators and jockeys. I remember going down to the start of a three-mile chase and being quite astonished to find a house jutting out on to the course, just where we were walking our horses round. I peered through the window, and there was a chap having his lunch, seemingly quite oblivious to what was going on immediately outside his front room.

Being particularly sharp and undulating, Cartmel is a course for specialists – and I mean jockeys as well as horses. You need to know all its eccentricities to ride the track properly, and no one was better versed in them than 'Big Ron' Barry, a giant among northern jockeys until he retired recently to a post as course inspector.

When Jonjo O'Neill first came to England, Ron took him under his wing and showed him the ropes. They became, and remain, very close friends, but Ron, who loves a laugh, would always get great amusement out of beating Jonjo at Cartmel. There is a very long run-in of about 500 yards, and Ron, having told Jonjo exactly how to ride the course, would then loom up on his outside halfway up the run-in, that familiar grin on his face.

One day, however, the roles were reversed. It was Jonjo, by now more experienced, who cruised upsides Ron, who was hard at work, pushing and scrubbing his beaten horse. Suddenly Ron leaned across and pulled the bridle up over the ear of Jonjo's horse. The Irish oaths could doubtless be heard from the stands. Jonjo still won the race – but literally, 'on the bridle', holding the bit in the horse's mouth to retain some control.

Knowing the two of them as I do, I have no doubt they laughed, rather than scrapped about the incident.

There are some jockeys who are seldom off the telephone, always ringing up trainers asking for rides. Others take the opposite, aloof stance and decline to phone anyone, instead waiting for their own phone to ring. I tend to steer a middle course, habitually contacting the trainers for whom I ride regularly, but seldom stepping out of familiar territory actively to seek outside rides. It has undoubtedly cost me winners but it might have brought me a certain peace of mind. It is, of course, still gratifying when a trainer phones to offer a ride, though I remember one occasion when the pleasure was somewhat confused.

It was in the middle of a quiet October, two or three seasons back. The trainer who rang was John Ffitch-Heyes, who has had considerable success with a smallish string in Sussex. I had never spoken to him before but I knew all about him. Sadly, despite the fact that it was him making the phone call, I was obviously not quite so familiar a name to John. Throughout the conversation, he insisted on calling me Stan!

Trainers vary enormously with regard to how much they say to their jockeys, both before and after races. Some can be seen giving pedantic instructions right up to the moment for mounting in the parade ring, then discussing every yard of the race immediately afterwards. Others say little, before or after, reserving their comments for more private places.

Brent Thomson, who made his name in Australia, encountered one of the first variety, early in his stay in Britain. Brent, a very capable flat jockey, had gone to Chester for the traditional May meeting, and his last ride of the day was his first for a particular trainer, who had better remain nameless. The parade ring instructions were detailed and prolonged, but amounted to the fact that he should make plenty of use of the horse, with the parting shot that he was expected to win.

The horse utterly failed to live up to his trainer's lofty assessment. Brent could not get him involved in the race at any stage and he finished tailed off. It happens – to the best- and worst-laid plans. For some reason, the trainer was held up coming off the stands and did not get down to the unsaddling area in time to see his jockey. His wife did, however, and proceeded to give 'B.T.' a furious lecture, together with an assertive diagnosis of exactly what he had done wrong. Now, even the most famous and accomplished of jockeys sometimes have to swallow their pride and their tongues to take such a rebuke from a respected trainer. A trainer's wife is a different story, and Brent was apparently not best pleased. He hurried away, changed quickly and was combing his hair in front of the weighing-room mirror when the trainer finally caught up with him. 'What went wrong out there?' the trainer asked, quite reasonably. 'You'd better ask your wife,' was the waspish reply. 'She seems to know a lot more about it than I do.'

One of the most irritating occurrences during a race meeting is when a horse spreads a plate in the parade ring. It is remarkable how often this happens just as the call comes to mount and, inevitably, it means a delay of several minutes. The jockeys and connections have to wait in the parade ring for the repairs to be completed and, by this stage, all instructions have been given and all pleasantries passed. The owners are usually nervous, the trainer a little anxious and the jockey – especially on a cold winter's day – is just eager to get on with the job and warm up.

This had happened during a flat meeting at Bath one day and Richard Fox, a very amusing and popular jockey, was standing with the connections of a hot fancy from the west country. Even the voluble 'Foxy' had run out of things to say when the delay extended to ten minutes and, in desperation, he turned to the fretful trainer and suggested: 'By God, guv'nor, if you've got this horse trained to the minute, as you say, I'm afraid he will have gone over the top by now!'

Sometimes, a request to ride for a particular person does not turn out at all as expected. I am thinking of a time when I was still apprenticed to Tom Jones and I was offered a couple of rides for a trainer named Len Carrod. He was, I can now appreciate, only a small-time trainer – a Welsh farming type who had a few horses somewhere near Market Rasen – but in my impressionable youth I was under the fond misapprehension that all trainers were wealthy enough to live in palatial houses. Consequently, when I had ridden for Len at Market Rasen on the Saturday and he offered to put me up for the weekend because he had another ride for me at Sedgefield on the Monday, I looked forward to a spot of luxury. Imagine my mortification when we arrived at the Carrod home – a four-berth caravan on a patch of wasteland. My quarters for the weekend comprised a sofa. We went to the local that night and I slipped away to phone my father and get him to find an excuse to pick me up. It might have seemed ungrateful, but it had been a lesson to me. Being somebody in racing is no passport to the riches of life.

Jockeys do not only seek their advice and instructions from trainers and owners. Very often, they get it from each other. One jockey, riding a horse for the first time, will ask the best method of riding him from someone who has been on the horse before; or, just as frequent, a jockey travelling out of his regular territory to an unknown course will seek some guidelines from a local rider, or simply someone familiar with the pitfalls of the place.

This was the scenario a few years back when Roy Mangan and John Suthern made the long trek from the Cotswolds up to Ayr to ride two horses in the Scottish Grand National. Roy, who was on a very good jumper, had been there before. John, poor chap, not only had to ride a notoriously dodgy jumper but had never so much as seen the course before.

All through the journey, Roy was teasing John, telling him that if it was the last thing he ever did he must be sure to get the horse over the first ditch as it was a particularly bad fence. He continued on the same tack in the weighing-room, and again down at the start, by which time John was thoroughly browned off and more than a little neurotic.

John was in the leading group as they set off, Roy holding up his horse in the rear. They cleared the first couple of plain fences without alarm and then approached the ditch, which in truth is nowhere near as intimidating as Roy had been mockingly making out. No matter – it was big enough and ugly enough to bring John's horse crashing to the floor. It was a terrible fall and Roy, following on, recalls that his heart was in his mouth as he saw the crumpled body of his mate on the landing side of the fence. All around the next circuit, he had the terrible suspicion that John was dead and that he had helped to kill him.

It is easy to imagine his relief when, just as the field approached that ditch for the second time, he saw John rise to his feet, a little stiffly, grimacing freely but apparently with nothing broken. It should also be no surprise that as Roy galloped past, turning a cheery grin of consolation to his pal, Suthern should shake his fist in a thoroughly unfriendly manner!

Injuries

Most people who lead ordered, sensible lives have a certain
ambivalent attitude to the onset of sickness or to the occurrence of an
accident. It may be unpleasant for a time, they reason, but at least it
stops them having to work. The doctor will sign a sick–note, the
money will continue to come in, and the feet can go up on the sofa
until full fitness is restored. I oversimplify, probably, but I happen to
know a good many people who do think that way. Jockeys simply
can't afford to. Even those, like myself, who have been fortunate
enough to have the support of a 'retainer', which is an annual fee paid
by the owners of a yard to ensure your availability for their horses,
cannot get by for long without any rides. The bread-and-butter
money comes from riding fees, the icing on the cake is win
percentages. If you are struggling to ride enough horses at all, let

alone enough who have a reasonable chance of winning, you are in trouble. I suffered this syndrome a few seasons ago; I had six weeks sidelined with a broken arm, then, when I was ready to crack on at full speed, my retaining trainer Nicky Henderson virtually shut down his yard as the horses were all struck by a debilitating throat infection. If I didn't actually have to wonder where the next meal was coming from, I certainly had to tighten my belt for a while, and it made me feel a greater sense of wonderment that there are so many middle-of-the-road jockeys in jump racing, scraping a living out of half a dozen rides a week and celebrating each winner as if it were their birthday. When jockeys in that bracket suffer an injury and find themselves signed off for a few weeks there is some genuine hardship.

Small wonder then, coming back to my original point, that jockeys react instinctively when they have a fall to pretend that things are not nearly as painful as they actually are. None of us enjoys being stood down from riding, and we will invariably do everything possible to persuade the on-course doctor that any injuries are very minor and in no way include a bang on the head – which means an automatic spell of rest.

No fall is funny, so I am not about to tell a stream of jokes about them. The situations which occur as a result of falls, however, can be well worth relating. No one during my career has suffered more severe injuries, nor treated them with such callous defiance, as Ian Watkinson. He was known as the 'Iron Man', and with every justification, as I think this selection of anecdotes from his falls file will reveal.

Ian's trademark, and his trouble, was that he would ride anything. Most of us, after a few years on the circuit and a share of scrapes with death and disarray, become a little choosy, turning down offers to ride a novice chaser with form figures of PFUF next to its name. Not 'Watty'. I am not sure whether he saw it all as a challenge to his man-hood or his riding ability, neither of which was ever in much dispute so far as I am aware. But, to the great delight of a good many north-ern trainers who might otherwise have been scraping the bottom of the barrel for a jockey, Ian never said 'no'.

As a perfect example of what I mean, he took a ride at Sedgefield one day on a twelve-year-old horse who was a notoriously dodgy jumper of hurdles but was now venturing over fences for the first time. The mixture seemed fated even before the tapes went up, but the old horse had clambered over the first few and was still in the race as the field passed the homely little grandstands for the first time and set off on the final circuit.

Disaster struck, ironically, on the flat. Approaching the next fence, four strides away and settled to jump it reasonably well, the old horse broke down. He took the fence on three sound legs and, as a result, was totally unbalanced. Crashing virtually straight through the top of it, he fired Ian out on to the far side of the fence and then, sickeningly, rolled all over him.

There were a couple of St John's Ambulance men, armed with a stretcher, by the side of the fence, and they sprang quickly into action. Ian was only semi-conscious as they loaded him on to the stretcher, but he remembers being surprised that they did not wait for the ambulance to reach them. Instead, they set off immediately back towards the main course buildings and the ambulance room. It occurred to him that they must want to get back to see the end of the race because, without any apparent need, they suddenly began to trot, bouncing the patient along on the familiar, none-too-comfortable canvas.

As they came off the grass of the course itself and on to the tarmac area at the side of Sedgefield's ancient stands, the St John's man bringing up the rear tripped and let go of his end of the stretcher. For the second time in a matter of minutes, Ian found himself hitting the ground rather hard. This time, he landed face down on the tarmac and broke his nose – which was quickly diagnosed as the only serious injury among a lot of bumps and bruises!

*   *   *

John Francome, the greatest jockey I have ever seen, retired from riding quite suddenly, one afternoon at Chepstow. The motivation for quitting, when he had previously been in no great hurry to pack up, was a horse fittingly called The Reject. John had previous bad memories of this talented but unpredictable chaser, but the end came when The Reject tried to refuse, throwing John sideways out of the saddle. His right foot, however, was still caught up in the stirrup – something which happens only occasionally but can cause the most excruciating ankle injuries. John literally hung alongside The Reject for a few seconds before thankfully disentangling himself. He came back to the weighing-room having made up his mind. That was the last time he would ever ride. A great talent was lost to the game, and I for one was stunned – although, once I had recovered from the shock, I was just grateful my old friend had taken the decision and got out in one piece.

A similar thing happened to Ian Watkinson a few years back. Predictably, his reaction was rather different. Ian was riding in a handicap hurdle at Wetherby, spurred on by the prospect of partnering that most spectacular steeplechaser Tingle Creek, later the same afternoon.

His hurdler was brought down. It wasn't a severe fall but, as the horse got to his feet, Ian's right foot was still stuck in the iron. Like Francome at Cheltenham, 'Watty' hung upside down, a long way off the ground. Instinctively, he grabbed for the horse's ear, the nearest solid object, but as the horse took fright and pulled his head away, the bridle came off in Ian's hands. Taking a chance, he spun his whole body and, fortunately, he went the right way. His foot came easily out of the iron and he fell to the ground, not feeling at all well. It was one of his regular problems – a dislocated knee – and from past experience he knew he had only twenty minutes before the knee would swell to twice its normal size and be all but immovable.

Now, I know what it feels like to miss a great ride through a freak accident, and I will always go to extremes to avoid it. However, if that had happened to me, and my knee was puffing up agonisingly, I think I would have accepted the inevitable and taken a couple of days off. Ian, in his headstrong way, was determined to ride Tingle Creek no matter the discomfort, and although he had to be helped into the paddock by the head lad, and virtually lifted on to the horse, he went through with it.

Tom Jones, Tingle Creek's trainer and the guv'nor to both Ian and myself at various times, was not at the races, which was probably just as well. Tingle Creek had only one way of running, which was to lead from start to finish; he was never headed early in a race and, more often than not, his spectacular, exhilarating jumping would take the opposition off its feet. On this particular day, however, and possibly because of Ian's handicap, Tingle Creek only occupied second place going to the first fence. He soon jumped to the front and went on to win, as expected, though with his jockey in terrible pain.

I know how bad Ian must have been feeling because he was forced to pull off the road on his way home and phone the guv'nor to ask for help. He found Tom in one of his more abrasive moods, however. 'He asked me if I'd made all on Tingle, as usual,' he recalls, 'and when I admitted we were headed going to the first he went mad and put down the phone on me. I didn't have time to ask him for a lift back.'

'Watty' battled back to Newmarket somehow. But the next morning, with the pain no better, he was forced to go to hospital for some painkillers and general treatment. By the time he arrived at the yard later that day, word had spread about his extraordinary courage (some would call it pigheadedness) to ride Tingle Creek in such discomfort. He met Tom walking across the yard. 'He asked me why I hadn't told him about the dislocated knee on the phone,' says Ian. 'I said he didn't give me much chance. What came next was the closest to an apology I ever heard from him.'

Ian's knee problems were a recurring topic of conversation in racing for some years. He had one cartilage removed but still he kept suffering dislocations. If you have done this more than once, the joint is always going to be weak, too weak for an activity as demanding as race-riding. Richard Linley, more recently, had a similar problem with his shoulder, which kept coming out of place; it helped him decide to take an early retirement and become a course inspector.

One Tuesday at Folkestone, Ian was literally crying with the agony after yet another dislocation of the problem knee. I had been riding at the same meeting and we went back to Newmarket together, by which time it was obvious he needed urgent treatment. It was quite late in the evening by the time we got him to his doctor's house, and, after giving him some pills to help him through the night, the doctor admitted him to hospital the following morning to have this second cartilage taken out.

Now this, remember, was the Wednesday, so you can readily imagine the astonishment of all at the hospital when Ian announced that, whatever they did to him, he wanted to be fit in time to ride the great Night Nurse in a big race at Ascot on the Saturday. This allowed three days for a recovery which, in those times, usually took four or five weeks.

It was Friday morning when, reluctantly, they allowed Ian out of hospital, the surgery completed but the stitches still fresh and evident. His first call was to Tom's yard. He rode a pony called Pansy once around the paddock, quite obviously biting on the bullet all the way. But, typically, he got off, limped across the yard and announced he would ride the following day.

The sequel to the story is the sort of thing that could only happen to Watkinson. Pumped up with painkillers, he won on Night Nurse. Not satisfied, he insisted on partnering Strombolus, a decent long-distance chaser, later on the card. Strombolus fell, and as Ian was pitched head-first into the ground, knocking him unconscious, the horse trod on his chest and broke his sternum!

It is a rule of mine now to take a day off on the Monday prior to the Cheltenham Festival. Unless a retaining trainer particularly asks me to ride one of his horses, which is most unlikely on this of all days, I will refuse all offers for the traditional meeting at Southwell. I have nothing against the place, it is simply that I am now old enough and wise enough to see the foolishness in putting at risk all the excitement Cheltenham has to offer just for the dubious privilege of riding a moderate horse on a country track. The lesson, I may add, was learned the hard way.

About a dozen years ago, when I was far more cavalier about the quality of horses I rode, a trainer phoned me to offer a spare ride in a handicap chase. I don't suppose I thought twice before accepting; I seldom did in those days. But, as will now seem inevitable, the horse took a bad fall and I emerged with a cracked collar-bone. I needed to bluff my way through the statutory inspection by the course doctor, I managed to escape being stood down, and decided that in spite of the considerable pain I would never forgive myself if I missed Cheltenham. So, the following day, I had the injury strapped up, I swallowed regular doses of painkillers and I went out to fulfil my engagements at Prestbury Park.

It was the second day of the meeting which really spurred me on. I was due to ride a horse called Sweet Joe for Tom Jones in the Sun Alliance Chase, and I was very hopeful that he would win. I had never previously ridden a big winner at the Festival so it meant a great deal to me, but, by the time the race began, the injection I had been given that morning, to deaden the raging pain from my collar-bone, had begun to wear off. I rode the race in agony, and although it was very much worthwhile, for Sweet Joe did indeed win, I made a promise to myself that I would never again take such a daft risk.

Ian Watkinson naturally has a similar tale to tell, typically rather more dramatic than mine. During the same Southwell meeting and of a similar vintage, Ian had taken a ride on a bad novice chaser which fell at the final ditch. The horse landed full on top of him, and the diagnosis was that Ian had broken his pelvis. The following day, his Festival rides were mouth-watering, including Alverton (later to win the Gold Cup) in the Arkle Chase and Sea Pigeon in the Champion Hurdle. Despite all the evidence to the contrary, he tried to persuade the course doctor that he had suffered nothing more serious than a few bruises. This tactic was made immeasurably more difficult when two doddering old ambulance men tried to lift him off the stretcher on to the bed in the medical room. The one holding his feet somehow dropped them at the critical moment leaving Ian hanging, half on and half off this raised bed, his eyes watering with the agony but scared to cry out for fear of revealing how serious the injury might be.

It was always going to be a lost cause. He might have conned the doctor but he could not con nature in this instance. I went round to Ian's flat the next morning at a prearranged time, ready to drive him to Cheltenham, but he was physically incapable of getting out of bed. He spent the next sixteen days in hospital, forced to lie in one particular position while the bone set. I don't suppose for a moment that even this heartbreak made him change his ways. He would have been back at Southwell on the second Monday of March the next year, taking any ride offered and giving it his best shot without a thought for what he had to come later in the week.

Ian and I shared a lot of good times together, but plenty of bad times, too. One week we even shared a hospital ward. It was the end of the racing season and both of us, ironically, required some knee surgery – Ian, because one of his many previous operations had apparently left him with the end of a surgical instrument inside the knee, and me because I had begun to suffer 'Watty's' traditional problem of dislocations.

It seemed a good idea to go in together and get the unpleasantness over with. The hospital even gave us neighbouring beds, doubtless consoling themselves with the thought that we would not be mobile enough to get up to any trouble. They misjudged us. The day after the operations, we were racing around the ward in wheelchairs, and I have a feeling the staff were very relieved to discharge us.

By then, however, I had discovered a thing or two about myself and operations. (1) I am a hard man to sedate – the first injection only knocked me out for a couple of minutes and they had to hurriedly give me another jab. (2) I am no different from anyone else when it comes to eating after anaesthetic. I woke up with a dreadful hunger and could not stop myself chomping through an apple by the side of the bed. It stayed down for all of five minutes and I quickly wished I had shown a bit more restraint.

Probably the best and certainly the most staggering of all the 'Iron Man' stories goes back to 1976 when Ian actually won a big race with a broken leg. Look up the form books for that season, find the entry for the Oxo National, a four-mile marathon chase at Warwick, and you will see that a horse called Jolly's Clump was the winner at 3–1. Behind that bare statistic lies a human drama. Ian had been so keen to ride the horse in that race that he had persuaded a doctor to set the broken bone in a splint and inject him with strong painkillers. How he got away with it, I shall never know.

The worst racing injuries are very often not caused by the most spectacular falls. A case in point is the day I broke my neck at Devon and Exeter. I was doing nothing more ambitious than steer a beaten hurdler through a convenient gap in the final flight, where one of the leading horses had flattened it, when quite freakishly he tripped on a loose piece of brush and catapulted me out of the saddle. I landed on my head and a stabbing pain shot up my arm. I knew it was nothing trivial (though I never suspected the truth) but in the normal way of things I assured everyone that I had only twisted my shoulder, because I was anxious to ride a couple of decent horses at Newbury the following day.

A good mate named Jamie Bouchard, a fellow jockey at the time, drove me back up the motorway route from Devon towards Newbury, where I intended to stop the night prior to getting some physiotherapy the following morning. Long before the Newbury exit, however, I realised that it was just too bad. Those good rides would have to be given up. I had to get home to bed.

Jamie drove me all the way to Newmarket and I saw a doctor the next day. He took some X-rays and telephoned me with the results some hours later. To say I was shocked would be a masterpiece of understatement. I had always imagined that a broken neck meant paralysis, a lifetime in a wheelchair. I felt bad, but I could still move. The doctor, however, explained that in a sense I had been lucky – the spinal cord had remained intact.

Exactly a year later I had a frightening case of *déja vu*. I was riding in the very same handicap hurdle on the corresponding Devon card. Again, I was approaching the last flight with no prospect of finishing in the places. Again, uncannily, there was a gap in the hurdle. The memories flooded over me and I spontaneously decided that nothing could persuade me to cross that hurdle. I pulled the horse up, invented some excuse to satisfy the trainer, and returned to the weighing-room with a strange sense of relief.

While I was recuperating from my broken neck, Ian Watkinson was also laid up. He was trying to get over the worst fall of his life, the fall which eventually finished him as a jockey. It has happened to many a rider and it will unquestionably happen again – the fearless 'Watty' simply had one fall too many.

It happened at Towcester, the final ditch in a chase. He was buried by the fall and did not regain consciousness for two or three days. A week or so later, he phoned me at about three o'clock in the morning, just wanting to talk. There was nothing wrong with his mind – indeed, his memory for incidents was amazingly sharp. It was just that he was convinced that things which had happened to us two or three years earlier had actually occurred the previous day.

I found it unnerving at first. I wasn't sure how to handle it. But, soon, we found a wavelength and the old camaraderie saw us through. We got over our respective injuries together, and one day, when we were both feeling considerably stronger, we went out to Sunday lunch. What with one thing leading to another, we got home again on the following Thursday. It didn't go down too well with the wives but you could say it was all down to my neck and his head.

The Grand National

I am not one of the most meticulous students of racing history, and nor am I a sentimentalist. Despite that, I have no hesitation in saying that the Grand National is the one race, year by year, which can bring a lump to my throat – it is also the race which throws up the most memorable stories, season after season, and you do not need to have a brilliant memory for most of them to be embedded somewhere in the subconscious.

No one who was there will ever forget Bob Champion's win on Aldaniti, in the year when the runner-up, old John Thorne on Spartan Missile, would himself have been an emotionally appropriate winner, too. The following year Mr Dick Saunders, at an age when most men are thinking of putting their feet up in front of the television come Saturday afternoon, rode Grittar to victory; then we had Jenny Pitman becoming the first lady trainer of a winner, Last Suspect belying his roguish reputation and imminent retirement, West Tip defying the ravages of a brush with death on the roads, and Maori Venture giving an overdue triumph in the race to his owner Jim Joel, well past ninety and still going strong. . . . These are just some of the highlights of the past few years, when I have been riding in the race. It would take a book by itself to tell all the stories – and, as quite a number have been written already, I shall not be trying to duplicate them.

Some readers might be aware that I have never won the National. Others might equally be aware that I have, however, managed to make headlines in the days surrounding the race. Aintree has not exactly been an uneventful place for me, and here I will try to recall a few of the amusing experiences along with some of the more painful ones.

Mention of the 1986 Liverpool meeting is sufficient to set off a shudder down my spine. This may seem odd to students of form rather than scandal; after all, I finished third in the National on Classified that year, a ride which I found so thrilling I can only imagine it was like being high on drugs without the mind-crippling side-effects. But that was the glossy side of the meeting, the sugar on a bitter pill. It was also the year that I got kidnapped in my car after a drunken night and – most culpably of all – allowed myself to tell the story on television. None of which, I later realised, was designed to increase my standing either with my boss, Nicky Henderson, or with his owners who pay my wages.

The story itself is now, unfortunately, pretty well known. I only wish it wasn't. Many found it hilarious at first, just as I did, but were later, quite rightly, to berate me for being irresponsible. I have no real defence to the charge. I am guilty. There were, however, at least some extenuating circumstances.

First among them was that I had just been beaten on a horse called River Ceiriog. Nothing special about that, you may feel, but you would be wrong. River Ceiriog, to my utmost surprise and delight, had won the Supreme Novices Hurdle at Cheltenham three weeks earlier, and, in my own mind, he was a certainty to get the Aintree meeting off to a successful start. I know, of course, that there is not really any such thing as a certainty in racing, especially at highly competitive meetings like Liverpool, but he had won so very comprehensively at Cheltenham that I could see no good reason for supposing he would not beat a very similar field again. He failed – not by much, in fact finishing second to Jenny Pitman's I Bin Zaidoon – but, in the grim mood into which I quickly plunged, a miss was as good as a mile. I sought solace in the company of some good friends, including a Scotch bottle, and by the time I got back to my hotel on the coast at Southport, I was if anything in an even darker frame of mind and ready to pick an argument with anyone. I take no pride in admitting that it was my girlfriend, Di, who caught the full fury of my frustrations, and I don't at all blame her for reacting as she did when I announced petulantly that I intended to go and have a few drinks with the boys back in Liverpool rather than taking her out to dinner. She told me I could find somewhere else to sleep that night and, after more drinks, so I did. I chose the back of my own car and covered myself with an overcoat. I did not lock the door – indeed, to my eternal shame, I have a feeling I left the keys in the ignition!

Many people will know how it feels to wake up and, in the semi-conscious state of early morning, to be uncertain where you are or why you are there. This dreamlike sensation is naturally exaggerated when one has had a few drinks the previous night; it is, and you must take my word for this, very much more pointed when you happen to wake up in the back of a moving car.

Fear, oddly enough, was not my initial instinct. It was outrage, mixed with bewilderment and indignation. I wanted to know why I was being driven along in the dark, in my own car – and by whom. Well, I never did truly discover why, but I discovered that the whom was a teenage youth, who must have had the shock of his life when I suddenly leaped out from under my blanket. He cannot have had any idea I was there and, if he had been a few years older, it might well have been cause of a heart attack.

My 'kidnapper' unleashed an appalling squeal of fright, put his foot down hard on the brakes and pulled clumsily across on to the hard shoulder before throwing open the door and leaving me without

so much as a farewell or a word of apology! I sat stunned and blinking for some minutes, trying to work out my next move. Thinking back, it did not even then strike me that I had just enjoyed a very fortunate escape. The youth might, after all, have been armed, dangerous or desperate – worse still, he might have had company. The consequences are too terrible to contemplate but, I repeat, I did not at the time stop to give them consideration. What most concerned me, having established that I was at an anonymous point on the M57, was that I was around twenty miles from Southport and in something of a dilemma. I either had to stay where I was, awaiting some very awkward questions when inevitably I was discovered by the police, or I had to attempt to drive back in a state which I recognised as something short of sober.

I chose the second option, took things carefully and pulled back into the hotel car park in Southport at about 4 a.m. Now, I had another problem. I still had no alternative bed, and as I could hardly go knocking on Di's door at this ungodly hour, pleading for a spirit of forgiveness she was not guaranteed to feel, I made the best of a very bad job and cagily settled down again in the car, having this time checked that all the doors and windows were locked.

Perhaps it was the sense of euphoria at such an adventure, such an escape. Perhaps it was just wanting to brag about something which seemed quite exciting at the time. Whatever the reason, I set about telling my friends all about the saga when I got to the races later that day. It was not long before it reached the ears of the BBC television team and, well, the rest is self-explanatory. Once you have told a tale on TV, there is no going back. You are stuck with it. I was front-page headlines on Grand National morning, for all the wrong reasons.

Already, some of Nick's owners were giving me strange looks and, no doubt, questioning whether I was the right sort of chap to be entrusted with riding their valuable horses. At least, that was what I imagined them to be thinking, and I can't say I blamed them. It is human nature, having read of revelries and escapades such as that, to believe that the fellow involved is something of a larrikin, and if there were those who suggested I might not be at my best on National day because of it, I had no answer. I knew it was not true, I simply had to go about proving it.

Sadly, having begun the day with a win on Kathies Lad in the two-mile chase, I was then surprisingly beaten on See You Then in the big hurdle event. This returned me to my mood of doom last experienced two days earlier, and I knew I had to lift myself rapidly and thoroughly if I was to make a go of the National, an unforgiving race in every sense. I think I managed it. I am proud of the ride I gave Classified and totally satisfied I could have done nothing more to help him win. But it did not end the story. There were recriminations, with Di, Nick and others, stretching on for days. It was a bad time, a time to take stock and reflect that, of all the daft things I have done in my life, maybe this was the most foolish. I have now given up staying in Southport and sleeping in cars!

Just to show that being careful is not the answer to everything, I relate the tale of the following year back at Aintree. Once again, my mount was Classified – this time, very well fancied by many people, including myself. I did stay at Southport, but very low-profile; those who saw me in the bar after nine at night were rare specimens. I was in bed early, in my own room, I argued with nobody and I turned up at the track on the morning of the race free of hangovers, headlines or any other assorted handicaps. It made no difference at all.

I was happy enough with our position after the first circuit and, as in the previous season's race, I began to creep closer as we went away from the stands for the second time. I was still travelling sweetly after jumping Bechers for the last time – the moment at which every surviving jockey gives a silent vote of thanks – but having crossed the next, disaster struck. Classified's saddle slipped right round to his left side, carrying me with it. I hung on for grim life, trying to drag myself back into the upright position, but the combination of the slippery saddle and the force of gravity was pulling me further and further underneath the horse. From this undignified position I could see the next fence looming. I had no wish to be a dead hero. I had no option but to let go and sink disappointedly to earth, left to count my sorrows at the breaking of the dream for another year. Twelve months seems a long time to wait and, at that particular moment, I feared I might never again have such a good chance of winning the race.

These days, I may be the exception to the rule – a rare reveller among a breed of calorie-watching, Perrier-sipping, eight-hours-per-night professionals. I don't say they are wrong, or that I am right . . . I do sometimes wish I had a little more company.

Time was when I would have been in the majority. A few years back at Liverpool, Roy Mangan, John Suthern and John Burke were in a party of racing folk who stayed up most of the Thursday night at the Holiday Inn hotel, drinking and playing cards. There had been a dinner earlier that evening and the guys were still dressed in their evening wear. Roy called it a day at about 6 a.m. but had only just dropped off to sleep when the phone rang. It was 'The Duke', David Nicholson, waiting in the lobby and demanding to know why one of his riders was late for the 7 a.m. departure for riding out. Roy recalls that he threw on his riding gear, rushed downstairs and managed to placate 'The Duke' while they waited for Suthern to do likewise. It was then that an apparition appeared at the door of the bar – Johnny Burke, still in his dinner suit, but plainly prepared to go straight to the course to ride his Grand National horse. Roy insists that not only did 'Burkey' beat them to Aintree, he also rode two winners later that day.

In my younger days, I could survive the late nights, down plenty of Scotches and still come up fresh as a daisy to ride the next day. Liverpool was my mecca, socially speaking; most of the jockeys from the south stayed up there, and three nights of high living were guaranteed for those, like me, who could stomach them.

I always used to stay at the Holiday Inn in the city centre, close to all the restaurants and clubs I liked to frequent. But, if I thought of myself as a nocturnal creature, I was a non-starter when compared to Tommy Carberry.

Now Tommy is one of the finest jockeys Ireland has ever produced. He was also an expert around Aintree, as evidenced by winning the National on L'Escargot in 1975. He did not, however, bother too much about sleeping. I vividly recall staggering back into the Holiday Inn at 3 a.m. one year, anxious to get four hours sleep after an especially hectic night. Tommy was at the bar, a half-drunk pint of Guinness in front of him and a few surviving mates around him. I marvelled at his staying power and went to bed. Shortly after seven, when I came down for a spot of breakfast prior to driving to the course to ride work, I was amazed to see Tommy still there, on the very same stool with a very similar pint of Guinness on the bar.

After a hard night on the town in Liverpool, I was not at my chummiest when I arrived at the course one National morning, a few years back, and attempted to park my car in my regular morning slot at the pub just outside the main entrance. For some extraordinary reason, there were car park attendants – complete with yellow plastic coveralls – on duty even at this early hour and one, a young man to whom I took an instant dislike, confronted me as I nosed my Datsun into the forecourt of the pub.

He was, even at his tender age, a typical jobsworth. He did not know why I could not park there at eight in the morning, but park there I could not. With my head feeling thick and my humour extremely low, I was somewhat short on repartee for this type of impasse, so after a few sentences of fruity debate I told him that if he did not get out of my way like a sensible chap I would run him over.

His answer was a leer, a disbelieving leer I thought. That was enough for me. I put my foot down and set off into the parking area. The youth, taken utterly by surprise, was swept up on to the bonnet, where he clung on for dear life, casting baleful, terrified and vengeful glares through the windscreen in rapid succession.

Eventually I applied the brakes a shade sharply, at which he predictably fell off in a heap. I parked the car and prepared to go about my honest business on the course, but the boy had not learned his lesson and, undeterred by what must have been a rare assortment of bruises, he rushed once more towards the car. I must say he was game. He threw open the door and pulled me out. He was bigger than me so I didn't struggle, instead concentrating on his intentions. He swung a punch and I ducked it. As he gathered himself to swing again I pulled the yellow coverall up over his shoulders, effectively incapacitating him. It was then no contest, and I was able to move on into the course with one battle won, if a little grubbily. Some will say my come-uppance arrived a few hours later. My National horse, well fancied, was carried almost off the course by a wild and out–of–control opponent at Canal Turn. He never recovered poise and fell two fences later.

The day Tommy McGivern retired from the saddle, racing lost one of its most vivid characters. Tommy was the archetypal Irishman; he would live life to the full, giving rein to his social nature, but when it came to business, he was a match for us all as a race-rider. I had some wonderful nights with him, both in his country and mine, and I miss his company.

I will never forget one year at Aintree when we were both riding horses with little or no chance – the type of horse, in fact, that I would think twice before even agreeing to ride in the National these days. Being Liverpool, and being McGivern, we had enjoyed a few drinks the previous night, and the race was going pretty much as expected so far as we were concerned. In essence, it was continuing without us; we were cantering round at the back, chiefly intent on negotiating the obstacles and coming back safe and sound.

As can happen on such occasions, I had begun to tell a joke. I can't recall now if it was a particularly good joke but it seemed to appeal to Tommy and we were having a good giggle going past the stands and out on to the final circuit. As we approached the ditch, the formidable third fence on round one, I was building up to the punchline, but suddenly I found I was talking to thin air. Tommy had fallen.

Oddly, my horse fell at the next fence, leaving me slightly winded. As I was lying on the turf, reflecting sadly on another Aintree flop, I was surprised to see Tommy sprinting up. I thought at first he had run the couple of hundred yards just to check on my health, but I should have known better.

'Jeez', he said, 'I thought I'd find you here. I knew you wouldn't leave me without finishing that story!'

For Brendan Powell, one of the great bonuses about riding Rhyme 'n' Reason to win the 1988 Grand National was the prize of a car which went to the winning jockey. Brendan, one of the quieter and more sober Irishman I have known (he insists he celebrated his win with a couple of glasses of Coke) was particularly in need of the prize because his own car had been stolen a few days earlier.

He does, I am pleased to report, show some Irish traits. Absent-mindedness can be numbered among them. For when, at the end of the day, he said his farewells and set off back down the motorway to his Berkshire home, Brendan failed to remove the board which the prize sponsors had attached loosely to the roof of the car to advertise their products and their generosity. Apparently, Brendan had only just nosed on to the M6, and was testing out his new acquisition with a little pressure on the throttle, when a tremendous crash alerted him to the fact that the board had flown off, endangering all traffic.

Social Scrapes

There are times when I have seriously wondered if I was born into the wrong age. My philosophy of life which, broadly speaking, translates to living for the moment, apparently sets me apart from most other jockeys of my generation. Some of them probably see me as a bit reckless, sometimes a bit foolish. I look at it another way – we are not on this earth for very long and it hurts me to let a day go by without getting as much enjoyment from it as possible.

Naturally enough, this attitude has led me into one or two scrapes in my time – regrettable when they happen but usually pretty amusing to reflect upon later. Some are frankly unprintable; others certainly ought to remain unprinted. Having put the lot through my private censorship scheme, however, I have managed to come up with a few anecdotes which should not cause too much offence.

Roy Mangan is a saddler now, running a compact, thriving business concern around the Midlands. As a jockey, he never made the big time but he was a decent horseman, a good, honest journeyman. I got to know him when we were both riding a good deal for David Nicholson, and he became a close friend. Roy was the type to share my outlook on life and, sometimes, to take it a stage further.

One night during the Cheltenham Festival, we had been drinking together in the bars and the marquees. As anyone who has ever been to the Festival will know, the after-race social scene is extremely lively and fairly prolonged, which is another way of admitting that Roy and I had probably sunk quite a few by the time we strolled into the car park. Whether that constitutes a complete excuse, I am not certain.

I was driving a Datsun at the time, and Roy, having clambered into the passenger seat, instructed me to reverse it up close to a white Rolls-Royce he had spotted nearby. Mystified at first, I soon followed the way his mind was working. It was, you see, a filthy muddy day and Roy's idea was to make it a little muddier.

It is, he told me, very easy to do. You put the car in first gear, then slam your foot down on the accelerator. The mud flies, and the car behind is in urgent need of a clean. The white Rolls was soon in a fearful mess and, deciding that this was rather fun, we picked out another couple of expensive white cars and gave them the same treatment.

We had no idea that the fourth car we selected belonged to Bob Champion. Nor did we know he was sitting in it at the time! The worst happened. No sooner had I manoeuvred the Datsun into position, selected first gear and shot forwards, than Bob opened his door and climbed out to see what was going on. The flying mud caught him squarely on his extremely smart suit. It also made a very good job of his car, interior and exterior. He was far from pleased. The next day he presented us with a cleaning bill which, somewhat shamefaced, we paid without argument.

Dirt and Roy Mangan were inseparable. His favourite trick, played on unsuspecting rookie stable-lads at David Nicholson's yard, had its base in the tack-room, an old barn with some horizontal beams. Roy used these beams for fitness training – press-ups and the like – but he also used them for a particularly filthy prank.

He made quite sure that he did his press-ups with his hands grasping the beams between two discreetly marked chalk lines. Then he would challenge one of the other lads to a competition to see who could do the more press-ups in a minute. What the other lad would not know, until it was too late, is that, outside his chalk lines, Roy had thoroughly smeared the beams with dogshit.

The jumping season traditionally starts in Devon, with a string of holiday meetings at both Newton Abbot and Devon and Exeter courses. To me, this is one of the most enjoyable times of the year. I base myself in the Palace Hotel at Torquay, where I am now very well known, and in between meetings I play a lot of tennis and do a lot of socialising. The racing is fairly relaxed at this stage of the season and I tend to treat August as a working holiday.

Inevitably, then, Devon has provided its share of stories, none more painful for me than the year I took a girl called Alex to the annual Start of Season Ball. After a few drinks and a spot of dancing I noticed another very attractive lady who appeared to be giving me the eye. I never have been much good at resisting that kind of temptation and, as I fancied her rather a lot, I did the unforgivable and changed horses in mid-evening, giving Alex the slip and taking my new partner back to the hotel.

The following morning, the room telephone rang. It was Alex. She was in the foyer. Apparently she had left her earrings in my car and wanted them back. Her icy tone suggested she was not amused by what had happened and I couldn't say I blamed her. With some trepidation, I went down to meet her, going over a few quickly rehearsed excuses in my head. I was faintly surprised to see she wasn't alone but, beyond noticing that her friend was middle-aged, solemn and carried a handbag, I paid her little attention. That was my mistake.

Alex called me a lot of names, as she was entitled to, and, after a few minutes of vainly pleading my case, I sensed she was about to take a swing at me with her bag. I grabbed both her arms to block the attempt and was feeling quite proud of myself when I was knocked to the floor by a crashing blow on the head. The other woman had slipped round behind me and hit the target with her handbag which, I can only assume, she had packed with lead.

Feeling extremely sore and now rather embarrassed as well (there had been a very interested audience in the busy lobby) I hustled them outside, passed on the earrings and hoped never to see them again. It was not, however, quite the last I heard of the fracas. The following week I was back in Devon for another meeting when Lorna Vincent, a good friend among the girl jockeys, smugly gave me a cutting from the local newspaper. The headline read: 'Jockey Struck in Hotel Foyer'. I knew the rest . . .

Another embarrassing moment in Torquay was provided by Richard Pitman's sense of humour. Ian Watkinson and I were checking into the Palace one autumn evening just as Richard and his then wife,

Jenny, were leaving. Richard, still riding at the time, had a twinkle in his eye as he came across to us, but I thought nothing of it. We didn't even see anything fishy in his insistence that Ian and I should have the room he and Jenny had just vacated. Something about a wonderful view. Not wishing to argue, especially as we had intended to save a few quid by sharing anyway, we readily agreed and told the receptionist. She instantly looked us up and down in a suspicious way but said nothing. The porter also seemed a little cool as he helped with our baggage. We soon found out why.

There was only one bed in the room we had requested. It was a large double bed. As the realisation dawned that Pitman had set us up, we protested to the porter, who rather dubiously went across to the room phone and rang down to reception. 'Those two blokes I've brought up,' he began. 'They say they're normal and they don't want a double bed after all.'

Same place, similar theme . . . Lennie Bennett, the comedian, was staying at the Palace one autumn at about the time when it was invaded by racing folk. Lennie was doing a summer season somewhere in Torbay, but he was not such a big name as he is now. Ian Watkinson, for one, had no idea who he was, which suited our prank perfectly.

A few of us were at the bar with Lennie one night. I'm not sure where Ian had gone but, in his absence, we persuaded Lennie that here lay an ideal outlet for his talents at camping it up. Suitably flattered, he agreed, and the next day he began his pursuit of the unsuspecting Watkinson, first introducing himself with high-pitched voice and limp handshake and then, whenever he came in sight, blowing kisses to Ian and poncing after him with exaggerated mincing steps. I feared he had overdone it, but 'Watty' took the bait, hook line and sinker. He was so scared of this rampaging 'gay' that he jumped into the swimming pool every time he approached. It was a pity to put him out of his misery but, after a few hours of this, the other guys were in such fits of laughter than even 'Watty' realised all was not as it seemed.

*   *   *

Still on the subject of things not being quite as they appear, I was driving back from a Saturday night meeting at Worcester a couple of years back, my foot hard down on the accelerator as I skimmed through the little town of Alecester, when I saw a strikingly attractive blonde, very expensively dressed, hitching a lift. This, I thought, was not an opportunity to pass up simply for the sake of getting home early. I stood on the brakes of my Porsche and skidded to a halt about twenty yards past the hitch-hiker, then waited in growing anticipation while the lovely creature trotted primly along the road and got in the car. In my defence, all I can say is that dusk was falling fast, for it was all a dreadful mistake. At close quarters I could see far too clearly that I was not giving a lift to a lissom and available female but to a bloke in drag.

There are quite enough pieces of gossip (much of it fanciful) flying around the racecourses with me as their central subject without my adding to them, so in general I have always tried to avoid mixing business and pleasure. I have failed, of course, as I now live with the daughter of my old guv'nor, trainer Tom Jones, and in my bachelor days I once sailed a little close to the wind by illicitly taking out the daughter of another, very prominent trainer.

After dinner in a decent restaurant we both got stuck into the liqueurs before going back to her place – which also happened to be the trainer's house – for a few more glasses of whisky. As tends to happen, one thing led to another. We ended up in bed where, some hours later, I woke up bursting for a pee. She gave me directions through the rambling corridors of the old house, and I could have sworn she said first right, and second left. I must admit, however, that I was feeling somewhat fuzzy-headed and, after bouncing off the walls along the way, I reached what I thought to be the bathroom door, threw it open and stood swaying, stark naked, in the doorway trying to accustom my eyes to the darkness.

Even in my semi-drunken state, I quickly realised that I was in the wrong room. This was not the bathroom, it was plainly a bedroom. What's more, it was Daddy's bedroom. There he was, this distinguished trainer, for whom I had occasionally been honoured to ride, lying there alongside his wife, while a young whippersnapper of a jockey, nude and inebriated after a night of passion with his daughter, stood staring at him.

I hesitate to imagine the scene if he had woken. His temper is notorious, under far less provocation. I slipped out as quietly as my condition would allow and thanked my lucky stars.

A few years ago, the idea of a British jockeys' team was hatched. Every other sport had its national team, so why not us? Foreign trips have followed, each subsequent summer, but none has been more ambitious or more memorable than the one which took in matches in three faraway countries – America, Australia and New Zealand – during a three-week tour.

We had a high-class team of five jockeys, and there was a tremendous will to win, to do well for the country and for the other boys rather than the usual selfish desire just to do well for ourselves. It did all of us some good, broadening our racing experience enormously. Needless to add, it was also extremely sociable!

In Australia, the media interest in us was quite phenomenal – far greater than we are used to back home. For ten days, we were made to feel like film stars, sifting the offers on interviews and TV appearances in between race meetings. Our 'fame' also attracted a number of female fans, and I began to get on particularly well with one of them. She, in fact, was in my room and performing a particularly pleasurable act when a phone call came through from a radio station in Adelaide. I had entirely forgotten my agreement to do a 'live' interview with them, but it was too late to back out now. The girl did not seem to notice and was certainly not distracted, so it may well be that I came over to some bewildered listeners in Adelaide as being somewhat breathless and excitable!

Jonjo O'Neill was a very popular team member on some of our early overseas trips, and I think he may even have surprised himself with his sociability. Very few people have ever seen Jonjo touch alcohol but, having persuaded him to get into the local spirit (excuse the pun) by sampling a shot of bourbon when we landed in America, I was amused at his discovery that he quite liked the stuff. He was still sampling it when we left four days later!

Jonjo, bless his heart, remained amazingly unworldly in a most delightful way. He was named in the team to race in Belgium one July, and we all gathered early in the morning at Luton airport for a short hop to Ostend in a privately chartered plane. The airline official came across to check our passports prior to take-off but received only a blank look from Jonjo. 'I thought as we were only going to Ostend I wouldn't need it!' he said. Fortunately, the official was very understanding of this baffling Irish logic, took Jonjo away to sign a form or two and then allowed us on our way to Belgium where Jonjo, his poise recovered, charmed the locals in his own inimitable way, both on and off the course.

I rode the 600th winner of my career at a Newton Abbot evening meeting one May. Quite by coincidence, Oliver Sherwood trained his 100th winner the same night, and the reasons to celebrate were amplified by the fact that his winning horse was Atrabates, which is owned by a very gregarious bunch of club cricketers from London.

Most of them were down in Devon for the night, and so, although my intention had been to head straight back to Lambourn, I was easily persuaded to stay on for supper at a regular racing folk's watering-hole called Diamond Lil's, in Torquay.

During supper I found myself next to Steve Taylor, a Lambourn-based journalist on the *Sporting Life*. We had agreed to drive back together, and he was a little taken aback when I asked him if he would like some poached salmon. When he said that it was one of his favourite dishes, I told him that I had some in the boot of my car and would let him have it later.

It was the early hours of the morning when we arrived back in Lambourn – too late to wake up my landlord John Francome. Steve offered me the sofa at his house, and before we went in I opened up the boot and watched his face fall as he looked down upon two of the biggest wet salmon imaginable. 'You told me this was poached salmon,' he said accusingly. 'And so it is,' I replied. 'Poached as in stolen, not as in cooked!'

The 'poached' salmon has been a standing joke between us ever since – but I can vouch for the fact that, whatever its origins, it tasted extremely good.

Pubs play a significant part in my racing memories. A lot of pubs, a lot of memories. But I doubt if any pub in the country evokes such happy, if hazy memories as the Fosse Manor, just outside Stow-on-the-Wold on the Fosse Way.

I used to go in there on a regular basis through the season – after racing, whenever I was in the area. But in March, at Cheltenham Festival time, I would be in there every night, virtually without fail. My routine, along with several other jockeys, was to change after racing, go to the cellar bar on the course (which no longer exists) and, after a few refreshments and several tall stories there, move on the twenty miles to the Fosse, reconvening for more drink and some food.

The landlord, whose name is Bob, is a racing man himself and unfailingly made us welcome, no matter how much noise we might make. There were times when the revelries among jockeys got a little out of order – Bob, for instance, has a photograph taken one night, pretty late, which features four bare backsides. From left to right, they can be identified as Roy Mangan, Philip Blacker, S. Smith Eccles and Richard Linley. All but myself have now graduated from the riding game and passed out into respectable society. Is there a moral here?

It was at the Fosse that I got into one of my most risky scrapes with the opposite sex. A jockey friend of mine had got married and I went along to the reception, which Bob was putting on in one of his back rooms. It was a particularly lively evening. I was married at the time, though only just, but I happened to get along famously with a girl who had better remain nameless because she was already pretty well-known in the racing world and was later to marry a trainer. One thing led, as it sometimes does, to the other, and the upshot is that I woke up with this girl in a local cottage I had persuaded a friend to lend me for the night.

As I had been due back in Newmarket the previous evening, I reasoned that I had better push along. In my haste, however, I could not find all my clothes. One item which remained missing was my underpants. They were reunited with me some days later . . . the lady concerned had posted them to me at home!

In recent years, the Fosse Manor has become one of the main staging posts for the Irish contingent of race-fans who annually invade the Cotswolds for the Cheltenham Festival. I confess I love the Irish. In fact, I almost believe I must have some Irish blood in me, because whenever I go there it feels as if I am going home. I have an affinity with the people and the way they live. Most of all, I suppose, I can identify with them socially – they are wholehearted revellers, and there are not many of us left in England any more.

Religion is no barrier to having a good time among the Irish – witness the number of priests cavorting around the betting rings and the bars during the Festival. Bob, the Fosse landlord, says he had a priest stay each year for the meeting. His name was Father Breen and, so the story goes, it was after him that the brilliant but ill-fated horse, The Breener, was named.

I have stood in the Fosse late at night bewitched by the antics of the Irish. Every now and again, on a particularly wild night, one member of the group will yell, 'The flag', as a signal for general orders of a particularly savage drink. The Irish flag is green, white and gold and it seems that if you mix creme de menthe (green), Irish Mist (white) and Bailey's Cream (gold) in a sherry glass, they will float as separate layers in an imitation of the flag. I tried one once – and only once!

Fergus Jones is an Irishman with a difference. Not only a good drinker, good gambler and good company, but a very good athlete, too. After a meeting at Naas, early one March, Fergus and some of his pals were drinking in a town pub when a group of athletes from across the border came in for a glass. They had, it turned out, been down to Cork for a sports meeting and were on their way home. Fergus saw a bet and bought them another drink.

Before too many glasses had been downed, Fergus had set up a race through the streets of Naas. He was going to take on the Belfast-based runners, with £100 at stake. The northern boys quietly had another drink – they knew how fast they could run. They did not, however, know how fast the deceptive Fergus could go. Needless to say, this bizarre race – which could not start until the main crossroads traffic lights turned red along the Dublin road – was won by Fergus, who added the £100 and the idea to his Cheltenham packing a week or two later.

His chance arose on the Wednesday evening in the Fosse Manor. A group of Hooray Henries, up from London for the meeting, were making a lot of braying noises in one corner of the bar. Fergus, adopting the shambling walk of a total drunkard, tottered over to their group and began downing their drinks. Incensed, they rounded on him. In his mock slurred voice, he stammered apologies and offered them the chance to take money off him in recompense.

It must have seemed too good a chance to miss. Within minutes, the race was set up and some substantial bets had been taken. Fergus collected several hundred quid and, mysteriously walking upright and speaking without slur, moved rapidly on to another pub to continue his evening's drinking in peace.

America

Back in the days when I was a freelance jockey and a married man (both situations destined not to last) the opportunity came up to spend part of the summer break in America. It was somewhere I had never been, and I jumped at the chance.

It all arose because I was the regular rider of a useful handicap chaser named Medoc, who won his share of races for Tim Forster. Medoc was owned by a rich American businessman by the name of Peter Thompson, who was then, and still remains today, one of the most astonishing enthusiasts for jump racing I have ever encountered. Peter has horses in his home country, of course, but he still owns a couple in Britain, notably that dour old mud-lover Knock Hill, who is in training with John Webber at Banbury. Virtually every time one of his horses runs in England, Peter will hop on a plane and fly across, spend a couple of nights at his favourite, very exclusive London hotel and fly back again. It would seem a mind-boggling undertaking to most people, but Peter is different – racing is his passion, he has no money problems and he cannot see why he should not follow his hobby in any way possible. Good luck to him, too, because it was through him that I first got to see the States and indirectly through him that the Great Britain jockeys' team made two visits to America five or six years later . . . but then that is another story.

I had won on Medoc two or three times during the winter of 1980 and Peter may just have been showing his gratitude when he asked if I would like a trip to the States, at his expense. If only all owners were as generous. . . . Anyway, after giving it some thought I decided that I did not much fancy going alone. I wondered if I was pushing my luck a little, but with Peter being such a character I thought he might not be averse to having two jockeys on his hands rather than one. So, next time he was in London, I took my good friend John Burke, one of the finest horsemen we have seen in recent years, down to have dinner with him. 'Burkey' must have said the right things, because, in no time at all, the invitation had been extended. Come June, and the season's end, we were on our way. It was, without doubt, the most eventful six weeks of my life, as the following selection of adventures may help to convey.

The 'fun' began as soon as we touched down on American soil. Washington, no doubt, has more than its share of terrorists and the immigration men seemed to have made up their minds that we were decidedly suspicious customers. Burkey's Irish passport was the real stumbling block, I suspect, and we were not allowed to proceed until a good deal of what I would have considered interrogation had taken place. It was mild compared with what was to come.

Peter was at the airport to meet us and a drive of several hours awaited us, down to his home in Easton, Maryland. Now Peter is not in the first flush of youth and he pleaded that the drive to the airport had tired him a little. I accepted the offer to take the wheel; rather looked forward to it, in fact, in Peter's generously sized limousine. And, for a good many miles, all went smoothly. The freeways were no problem, even to a stranger such as me. It was when we cruised into suburbia that I began to hit problems.

There seemed to be a set of traffic lights every few hundred yards. As by now I was getting a bit tired myself, and as the company was not very lively – both passengers were fast asleep – I found it all a bit irritating. I noticed that American traffic lights lingered rather longer than ours on amber and quickly got into the habit of taking them on. At one major junction, I had my foot down, fully committed, when the amber light turned red. I kept going, and within seconds I thought the full wrath of the state police was descending upon me. Sirens were wailing, lights flashing. It was like a scene from 'Miami Vice'. I gave up gracefully and pulled over.

In England, the routine on being stopped for a traffic offence is to get out of the car and talk things over with the friendly officer. Apparently, the ground-rules are different in the States, and you are supposed to sit right where you are, with your hands on the wheel, until told to move. Not being aware of this, and not having Peter (still sound asleep) to warn me, I jauntily leaped out of the car and prepared to put up a very plausible defence as a foreigner unfamiliar with American traffic lights. I was not given the chance. To my surprise and alarm, I found myself spreadeagled across Peter's car, hands pinned above my head, staring down the barrel of a very menacing .45 gun.

Heaven knows what would have happened next. Fortunately, the commotion had finally roused Peter, who emerged from the passenger door to make the necessary explanations. With rather poor grace, I thought, the officers allowed us to go on our way, Smith Eccles thoroughly shaken. At that particular moment, I think I would happily have taken the next plane back to London.

I don't believe in ghosts . . . at least, I used to think I didn't. After a couple of nights in Maryland, I was revising my opinions on the supernatural and coming to the conclusion that there must be something in it after all.

Following that brush with the traffic police, I was very grateful to see journey's end and Peter's home, which turned out to be a substantial mansion. The drive, sweeping up towards the house, seemed to be all of two miles long; behind the house, vast grounds led down to what Peter described as his 'creek', but to me looked much more like a very wide river. It was a marvellous place, and I began to think that Maryland might not be so uninviting. Once Peter had poured out a generous measure of Scotch, I quite began to enjoy myself.

The evening was already pretty advanced and all of us were tired, so it was not too long before rooms were allocated and 'Burkey' and I crashed out for the night. I was in a room opposite John, a room which Peter had been quite insistent I should stay in. It struck me at the time as being a little odd but, with sleep the priority, I thought no more about it.

I spent a restless night and, afterwards, found it impossible to explain why. When admitting at breakfast the next day that I had not slept well, I instinctively put it down to jet–lag and even felt tempted to believe it, as the natural answer. I knew, however, that I had never experienced that sort of jet-lag before; I had felt weird, un-comfortable and insecure.

Even that did not in any way prepare me for what happened on the next night, a night I don't think I shall ever forget for as long as I live. We had gone off to bed at a decent hour, and after no more whisky than usual, but I had not been in bed long when the room temperature appeared to drop alarmingly from comfortably warm to ice-cold. Now, I know this sounds ridiculous, I know that all logic says it cannot have happened and that most people will assume I was drunk. But it was all too real to me and, if I had drunk a few Scotches, I was suddenly as sober and alert as I have ever been, for I felt the definite sensation of a hand, a cold hand, on my leg just above the ankle. It was pulling me down and out of bed and, unashamedly terrified as I was, I followed my instinct to fight whatever it might be. I struggled into a sitting position and started to throw punches blindly – all, of course, to no effect. I then rushed out of the room, half-dressed, and blundered across the corridor into John's room. When I told him what I had felt, he plainly thought I had gone mad but, interestingly, refused my offer to go in and find out for himself. I occupied the spare single bed and we shared a room for the rest of our time at the Thompson mansion.

A couple of mornings later, I had left the house early to ride out for one of the local trainers. 'Burkey' was alone at the breakfast table when the maid, an ample black woman of formidable appearance, came in and asked him why my bed was not being slept in. Slightly hesitantly, he told her that, in essence, I had come to believe the room was haunted. She, apparently, gave a slow smile of understanding and began to tell a story.

When the house was first built, so the story went, the owners had two young sons. Doubtless, it was a paradise for adventurous boys to grow up in such surroundings, but tragedy struck this family when one of the sons developed appendicitis. This, remember, was a good few years ago, in the days when appendicitis was a particularly serious illness. Doctors decided an operation was necessary but they failed to save the boy. It was the pay-off which sent a shiver up my spine, when John related the story to me later in the day. The operation had been carried out in the house, indeed in the very room I had been allocated as a bedroom. The boy had died there and this, evidently, was by no means the first time he had been back to haunt later inhabitants.

After a week or so staying with Peter, our plan was to move on to Saratoga, chiefly to find some riding work but also to see a little more of the country. Peter happily fell in with this scheme (he had probably had quite enough of us by then anyway!), and, as we didn't have our own transport, he suggested that he should take us to a day's racing at Belmont Park, outside New York, from where we would be able to get a lift.

Having said our farewells at Belmont, we initially thought we would settle for a night in the racecourse stable-lads' hostel. When we looked at the accommodation, we very rapidly changed our minds. It was absolute squalor, three or four lads sharing each room with a tiny bathroom attached. I don't think English stable-lads would have put up with it; English jockeys certainly didn't intend to.

We asked directions to the nearest hotel and put up there. This, too, was hardly the Dorchester. The fact that their charges were sixty dollars for a night, but thirty dollars per room for two hours, made it perfectly plain what kind of joint it was. But, as it was only for one night, and we had a lift aboard a horsebox to Saratoga arranged for early the next morning, we were not too fussy.

With a few hours to kill and nowhere in particular to go, John and I wandered out into the half-light of the evening in search of a bar. At the end of the road was a T-junction. Without any particular discussion or indecision, we turned right, quickly chanced upon a bar and settled down with a couple of Scotches. It was a rough and ready place, though no worse than many I had been in around the world, so I was slightly surprised to see a burly guy at the bar wearing a sinister-looking cosh strapped to his leg. He turned out to be a taxi-driver, and the cosh turned out to be his passport to getting through the day. He asked us, conversationally, which way we had come; equally conversationally, he said we had made a very wise decision. If we had turned left instead of right, he added with complete certainty, nobody would ever have seen us again. That T-junction apparently marked the divide between marginal safety and black gangland. Quite by accident, we had saved ourselves.

We left Belmont in the horsebox in the pitch dark of the early hours, and dawn was still only just breaking when we pulled into the famous Saratoga course, scene of so many American dreams, made and shattered. 'Burkey' and I were peering out of the window across the course; there were a number of horses out at exercise, but the first to catch our eye was cantering quite close to us. Simultaneously, John and I let out an exclamation of disbelief. We had come all this way, thought we knew nobody in the vicinity, and the first man we see on horseback is none other than our riding mate back home, Richard Linley.

Even in the mist, his riding style was unmistakable, but I imagine he was frightened out of his early-morning reverie when two unshaven heads poked out of this horsebox rumbling past and yelled 'Skinner' (his popular English nickname).

It transpired that Richard had rented a flat over a restaurant, very close to the Saratoga course, and was earning a buck or two riding out in the mornings, with the rest of the day to himself. Luckily, two more flats in the block were vacant, so we pretty much turned it into an English jockeys' hostel. The next fortnight was lively and convivial; the one part I soon decided I didn't much care for was the work.

'Skinner' showed us the ropes, which consisted of getting up at the ungodly hour of four o'clock each morning and walking around the barns at the course (most trainers in America are based on racecourses rather than on their own private premises) asking if anyone was short of a work-rider. All of the head-lads were black, most of them seemed to me to be understandably surly at that hour and, uniformly, they appeared to consider us three totally mad Englishmen. I soon gave up and went back to bed, emerging very little on future mornings, but John was a bit strapped for cash so he persevered until he found a trainer with a vacancy.

Richard Linley had a pretty regular job riding out for a South American trainer who was confined to a wheelchair. 'Skinner' told us that each morning, while he was tacking up his horse before exercise, the trainer was pushed into the box by an enormous negro. Soon, he said, he felt as high as a kite because the trainer was forever smoking joints.

Fed up with having to beg lifts or walk, we went to the local rent-a-wreck establishment and hired ourselves an imposing old Cadillac. There was plenty of room for all three of us on the wide, bench front seat, and we had some fun in that car even if it had seen better days. I discovered, however, that the Americans are very possessive about their trees, if not about their cars. One day on the racecourse, setting off for a lunchtime drink in too much of a hurry, I reversed the car into a sapling and flattened it. I'm told it was the one sapling they boasted at Saratoga and apparently they were rather proud of it. The police took a dim view of the incident but I got by somehow with the 'innocent foreigner' line again.

John Burke and I palled up with a couple of Yanks who worked on the racecourse. They were rough and ready types, but plenty of fun to be with and never short of an idea which might land us in trouble.

One day, they decided we should have an outing on the Hudson River – you know, gently cruising downstream with a few beers to pass the time . . . at least, that is how I imagined it. I was soon to be disillusioned.

We took two cars, stopping at a village on the way for the beer. It was the other purchase which puzzled me – the Yanks insisted we each bought a rubber tyre inner tube, suitably inflated. When they explained what it was for, I began to get the picture and realise that we were not about to have an afternoon of lazy luxury.

Leaving one car in the riverside village, we all piled into the second vehicle and drove five or six miles upstream before embarking on our 'cruise', which involved sitting in the inner tubes and floating with the tide. Somewhat to my surprise, I found it was not at all a bad conveyance. With the beers balanced precariously in front of us and a good deal of chatting and laughter going on, time passed companionably enough until, maybe a mile downstream from our starting point, we heard an ominous roaring sound just around the next bend and, helpless to prevent it, we found ourselves tumbling down some rapids.

If I had known what was coming, there is no way in the world I would have been persuaded to get inside that tyre. As we were thrown down the white water, flying across huge boulders, I looked up briefly and caught a fleeting but unforgettable glimpse of 'Burkey' with a look of abject terror on his face.

Somehow, we all managed to stay on board, although the cans of beer were gone forever. Back in the relative peace of flat water, laughter came quickly again – more as an intoxicated release than because any of us had found it particularly funny. If we thought the excitement was over, however, there was a shock in store. A mile further on, we hit the big ones, and these appeared to go on without end; we dropped into what seemed bottomless holes, bounced off the rocks and lurched into each other. My arms were clinging to the tube, my utterly inadequate lifeline, and I remember to this day thinking that I was about to die.

Once again, though, we reached the end. This time, nobody laughed for a while. I inspected my arms and found that the biceps were now raw, the skin torn off by the rocks. That apart, however, the physical damage was confined to a few bruises. I was grateful to get out of that rubber tube and get my legs working on terra firma again . . . but at least I can truthfully say that I have shot the rapids on the Hudson River.

Spectators

Racing attracts many different types of spectator. There are those who go racing because they are in some way involved, there are those who go simply for the thrill of the sport, there are those who go because it is a socially acceptable pastime in their particular society. And then, of course, there are those to whom a day at the races is nothing more or less than an orgy of betting which will begin with an utter conviction that a stack of money is about to be made and will end, more often than not, with empty pockets. Most racegoers bet to some extent, of course, but I am not referring to those who simply punt a few pounds to add interest to their afternoon. I mean the type who is much more interested in the betting than the racing itself. This can be a dangerous breed, a potential health hazard to jockeys.

A lot of heavy, habitual punters are not very gracious losers. Many of them, I suspect, cannot afford the sums they are plunging into the bookies' satchels and, when they back a loser, they begin to talk through their pocket – often with the benefit of a substantial alcohol intake just to raise the decibel level. They are at their most dangerous when they have backed a short-priced favourite, an apparent stone-cold certainty, and it has been turned over. It happens every day for no reason other than the favourite not being at his best or, equally likely, an unfancied horse running very much better than his price would indicate. But try telling that to a slightly inebriated, extremely angry punter who has just wasted his week's wages and is intent on taking out his wrath on the nearest available target – usually the jockey. To this type, a jockey who gets beaten on what seemed a good thing is undoubtedly a crook.

Jockeys tend to avoid racecourse bars if they have had a particularly bad afternoon and maybe been beaten on a couple of favourites. It is not shame, or guilt, which drives them away, but a sense of self-preservation, an anxiety to avoid the sort of ugly confrontations I have seen rather too often. Sometimes, however, even staying out of the bars is no guarantee to safety. A few years ago at Plumpton, a Sussex track which invariably attracts trainloads of cockney punters with more mouth than manners, David Mould was the target for one of the most menacing uprisings I have seen. It was the usual thing – an odds-on shot which failed to oblige – but the roughnecks of the betting ring were in no mood to listen to excuses, however valid. David was very relieved to get back into the weighing-room, but, as the fracas continued outside, his dilemma then was how he was going to get out again. Eventually, the police smuggled him out of the back door and escorted him to his car, which was luckily still in one piece.

In my time, I have seen and heard of jockeys having beer cans, toilet rolls and racecards thrown at them by the ugly element of race fans. I think I can do better than that: I would be pretty certain I am the only rider who has, on separate occasions, been the target for (a) a handful of coins, and (b) a dustbin.

The money rained down once at Market Rasen, at an autumn meeting. It was a three-year-old hurdle and I was riding a horse called

Dhofar for my Newmarket neighbour and good friend, Gavin Pritchard-Gordon. Like most of Gavin's jumpers, Dhofar had been useful on the flat and was later to become a very decent hurdler. Gavin had planned an early campaign for him, as he enjoys the fast ground, and he was sent to Market Rasen to bid for his second win in five days. The bookies had no doubt whatever, and neither did the punters. By the time the tapes went up, he had been furiously backed to a quite ludicrous price of 5–1 on.

Although I don't think any raw young hurdler merits that kind of price, especially in those muddling, early-season races, I have to say I thought he was pretty near a certainty, because I could see nothing in the relatively small field which should get close to him. I had, however, reckoned without a northern-trained animal called Tommy Gunner. He never reproduced the form in later races, and he may only have been moderate anyway, but the fact remains he beat my horse by four lengths, fair and square.

It might be that Dhofar was suffering from two races in rapid succession; it might have been that he took a dislike to the track. He might simply not have been feeling at his peak – a contingency punters often fail to even consider when discussing why a favourite has been beaten. Whatever the reason, it was an unexpected reversal and I was not feeling at my chirpiest as I walked Dhofar back up the track and through the trees towards the unsaddling enclosure.

Quite without warning, a tall, aggressive-looking guy suddenly yelled: 'You crooked bastard, Eccles', and, without further ado, hurled a handful of coins at me. The range was alarmingly close, the accuracy only marginally faulty. The coins hit poor old Dhofar, who shook his head in momentary fright and then plodded on for the inquisition. I was part angry, part relieved. I had been literally a sitting target and any one of the coins could have taken an eye out.

There was a policeman on hand, near enough to have witnessed what had gone on, and the man was rapidly pounced upon, interviewed and, I believe, charged with some public order offence. It was not, however, the last I saw of him.

I was driving out of the course at the end of the afternoon when I saw the guy walking along the road in front of me. Drawing slowly alongside, I wound down the window and called out to him: 'Did you do your money, then?' After a moment of bewilderment at being hailed from a strange car, he focussed clearly enough through what was probably a drunken haze to recognise me as the cause of his tantrum. By the look on his face, he was quite prepared to have another shot at hitting me with anything which might have come to hand. I did not wait to find out. My car always did have decent acceleration.

Uttoxeter, the quaint little course in rural Staffordshire, was the scene of the dustbin incident, and although the circumstances were slightly different, the motives for assault were just the same – a punter acting through the hole in his pocket.

It was, as I remember, a Bank Holiday meeting, which is probably why I had gone there to ride quite a number of favourites. Not that I mind Uttoxeter – my parents live nearby, and racing there is always an excuse to drop in at home and have myself fattened up by my mother's cooking! There is also a friendly atmosphere about the place. It is frequented by farmers, country-folk, proper National Hunt sorts. On that particular day it was also frequented by a dangerous headcase.

I might have guessed what sort of day it was going to be when the first of my fancied rides broke down, right in front of the stands. I knew instinctively that he was seriously hurt, as a jockey almost always does, and I pulled him up accordingly. To those in the stands, especially those who know more about betting than about horses, I suppose it might have looked a shade suspicious, but nothing could be farther from the truth. Firstly, I had made the trip to Uttoxeter specifically because I thought I might ride a few winners there. Secondly, if a jockey did want to get a favourite beaten, I cannot believe there is a more foolishly obvious way of doing it than pulling up in front of the main stand!

Anyway, with that little disappointment behind me, I went out for the next event, a three-mile chase in which there were only four runners. Once again, I was on the favourite and, once again, things did not go exactly to plan. Coming up the straight to the bend before the stands, a circuit still to run, I was last of the four runners. There was a long way to go and, although I was not getting the signals I would have liked from the horse beneath me, I was far from panicking at such an early stage.

You can, then, imagine my surprise when, out of the corner of my right eye, I noticed a man pick up a dustbin, take careful aim and hurl it over the running rails directly towards me. His 'present' was accompanied by another rendering of: 'You dirty, crooked bastard'.

If the dustbin had been empty, I think it would have hit either the horse or me. The aim seemed pretty good. Fortunately, he had chosen to throw it fully loaded and, while rubbish flew in all directions, the bin itself dropped gratifyingly short of us.

I suppose one can react in a variety of ways to this sort of thing. My instant response was to laugh. In fact, I was seized by such a fit of laughing that it was all I could do to keep my horse on a relatively straight line.

The police arrested the culprit and, as I suspected, it turned out that he had backed my first beaten favourite, lost most of his money and then, at the sight of me trailing the field on another favourite, entirely lost his head, assuming I was up to all kinds of tricks. I don't think he is welcome on that racecourse any more.

Mucking In, Mucking Out

Racecourses are the shop window of our game; jockeys could be thought the window display. But the warehouse, where the goods are produced to order and where the great majority of the real work takes place, is the stable-yard. It is here that the trainer will fret over each of his equine charges, day by day, where jockeys like myself will come to ride work and school the horses on the gallops, and, just as important, where the well-being of all the horses is catered for by a team of hardy specimens, male and female, age no barrier but all under the loose title of stable-lads.

Stable-lads are to be admired for their resilience and respected for their memories. As a jockey, I have very often been on the sharp end of some reproachful words from a lad (or lass) with crystal-clear recall of a bad ride I may have given his/her horse in the dim and distant past. As a general rule, they regard the two or three horses in their personal care with the possessive affection a parent would give to children, and anyone who might in any way abuse one of their animals is in for a very rough ride. This type of aggressive loyalty is, of course, responsible for sustaining the British racing game in its hectic, six-days-a-week, fifty-two-weeks-of-the-year routine. Without stable-lads, and their dedication, there really would be no racing.

If I say they come in all shapes and sizes, I really am serious. Many stable-lads, it must be said, are frustrated jockeys, who may either have been lacking the shape, the strength or perhaps even the skill to make the grade in the highly competitive riding market. It is to their credit, I believe, that they remain in racing in what many would regard as a relatively menial role. I don't think I could ever have done that if racing had not treated me quite so well. By saying that, however, I don't mean to give the impression that the stable-lad's life is all thankless slog. On the contrary, they are a band with a common interest, a unique existence and, inevitably, a lot of fun.

There are things which happen in stables every day of the week which cause a laugh. Some don't translate very well to paper. In this section, however, I shall recount a few tales from the backroom of racing – some involving lads, some featuring my own jockey pals, but all centred on the HQs of racing, the stable-yards.

Rod Simpson, now a clever and popular Lambourn trainer, started out as a stable-lad in Epsom, attached to Cyril Mitchell's yard. After two and a half years with Cyril, who is father of the current Epsom trainer Philip, Rod moved on to join Frank Muggeridge in Crawley. Frank was only a middle-of-the-road trainer, but I'm told he could have been among the really big boys if he had been more ambitious. I can think of others in my generation who must be of similar outlook – content with their lot and not very interested in expanding their operations to a point where life is constantly high pressure. Frank Muggeridge, however, still had some capable horses and Rod was happy there because he had been granted a licence to ride.

To a stable-lad, this is a passport to Utopia. It is no guarantee of riding every week, much less every day, but it is tangible encouragement, living hope of occasional escape from the background routine into the spotlight. Licences are highly prized and Rod, inevitably, attracted some jealousy among those lads who had little or no hope of ever getting a ride. Among these was a lad named David, ostensibly a friend, but very much an enemy when it came to racing.

Those who know the Rod Simpson of today, with his colourful dress sense, may not be entirely surprised to learn that back in the 1960s, the teenage Rod was a Mod. He rode around on a scooter, and needed it each day as he was still living at home in Croydon – twenty-two miles from the Muggeridge stables. It meant an early start and a late finish, and Rod had a regular routine he followed faithfully whenever he was to go racing. After riding out in the morning, he would change into his smarter clothes at the stables, packing his dirty gear onto the back of his scooter before setting off for the course. When he got back to the yard after the meeting, he would simply slip on a parka jacket, jump on his scooter and ride home, where the dirty clothes would be rapidly deposited in his mother's washing machine. It was an ordered, sensible routine, and, doubtless, it was well known to all the other lads in the yard.

At this point in the narration it is necessary to inform you that the Muggeridge yard was not only in the business of breeding and racing horses, but also of breeding rats. Big, black ugly rats, of a type which would make my stomach turn, I have to admit. Stable-lads being what they are, however, saw this as decent, wholesome sport; they would pinch some of the horses' feed and put it down in the holes around the tack-room, fattening up the rats for later capture.

One day, Rod had to go racing with one of the horses in his care. He followed his usual schedule, dumping his washing in the machine at home and thinking no more about it. It was the following evening that he arrived home from the yard to find his mother in a filthy temper, almost beside herself with rage and, he sensed, a shade of fright. She informed Rod that the washing machine was clogged up and that he must go and see what he had caused.

Mystified, Rod went to inspect the washer and, other than an awkward tangle of clothes inside, he could see nothing wrong. His mother, struggling to contain herself, ordered him to dig out his racing clothes. When he did, out flopped the dirtiest, biggest rat he had ever seen. Rod swears it was all of eighteen inches long and proportionately fat. He says he could well imagine the horror with which his mother had been obliged to watch this creature whizz round inside her washer, the front window giving the image of a particularly lurid late-night X-film.

Having made his peace with his mother, Rod set about confirming his suspicions that the villain of this act of treachery was his old protagonist, David. It did not take him long, stable-lads being notoriously bad keepers of secrets. David, who apparently went by the nickname of 'Barney Rubble' due to his facial similarity to the character in The Flintstones, was confronted in the corner of the tack-room and was told in no uncertain terms that he might have caused Mrs Simpson a major heart attack.

Rod, however, was not satisfied with mere detection and verbal reprimand. He wished to conduct a vendetta of revenge and, over a period of days, an equally foul plan was brought into being.

It was mid-winter, cold and bleak everywhere, most of all on the exposed gallops of racing stables. David's answer to the conditions was to bring a flask of soup to work each day. In his eagerness to get at the warming liquid, he was habitually first into the tack-room after riding out. Having observed this phenomenon Rod moved into action. One morning he arrived at work, sought out the head lad and pleaded that he felt too ill to ride out first lot. Explanation duly accepted, he watched the string leave the yard, David astride one of the horses, and then scuttled around to the back of the house where he knew of old there lurked a particular breed of toad.

Being a resourceful young man, it took Rod only a matter of minutes to collect three toads, stuff them into the pockets of his coat and run back into the tack-room. He then quickly located David's soup flask and (switch off here if you fear you might be offended) stuffed the toads inside.

An hour later, the string returned and, as usual, David was first into the warmth of the tack-room. Rod sat quietly in the corner, still complaining of sickness but secretly excited as the scene unfolded. Opening his flask, David tipped it up to pour the soup into a mug and found he could get only a few drops out. Without looking inside it, he turned the flask upside down and whacked it on the bottom, much as you would to get the sauce out of a ketchup bottle. It was an overwhelming success. Out came a mutilated toad, and then another, falling in the astonished David's lap. He took one eye-popping, horrified look to make sure he was not imagining things and then promptly passed out on the floor.

It had been a savage revenge. The boy David apparently needed a stomach pump at Crawley Hospital as a precautionary measure. But he never troubled Rod again.

It says rather a lot about Arthur Stephenson that, on the day when he won the Gold Cup with The Thinker in 1987, he was several hundred miles away, saddling a few runners in some obscure races at remote Kelso. Arthur is an oddball among trainers, an introspective type who would far rather stay out of the spotlight and allow his horses the chance to do his talking for him.

The fact remains, however, that W.A. Stephenson is among the most consistently successful of trainers – around the country, not only in the slightly less competitive north – and if he is regarded as an eccentric by some of the more conventional of racing types, it is no bad reflection on his ability.

It is impossible to have a social conversation with a group of northern jockeys without Arthur's name cropping up. This is chiefly because so many good jockeys have passed through his yard, as stable-lads, conditional riders and then retained jockeys. Chris Grant is the latest to have the pick of the Stephenson horses and, in terms of the chance to ride winners, there are very few better jobs in the country.

Arthur's lads do not boast about being the smartest in the country. Formal clothes are apparently not essential in the County Durham yard, where, it would seem, the only thing that matters is producing the horses spot-on for their next run. I hear tell that Arthur, who is now pushing seventy, has not spent much time on the morning gallops for some years now and that his lads have occasionally taken advantage, disobeying his express instructions by linking up with the local hunt, aboard some of the yard's prime racing stock. This allegedly went undiscovered until one of the horses, over-animated during the hunt, ran straight into a telegraph pole and was instantly killed. There was no hiding–place for the lads that day, and I guess Arthur may subsequently have been rather more vigilant whenever the hunt has been around.

Of all the tales I have heard about the Stephenson yard, however, the one I like best concerns a horse called Super Mikado, who was, by all accounts, a candidate for the equine lunatic asylum. As ever with such disreputable beasts, Super Mikado was looked after by a lad (in this case a girl) who doted on him, refusing to listen to the hateful words of others. She pandered to his every whim and was predictably distressed when, one winter morning, she was following the guv'nor's instructions to 'lunge' the horse around the paddock and the rein broke. Not being one to miss such an opportunity, the horse bolted into the middle distance, sketchily clearing a five-bar gate several hundred yards away and then promenading at a good pace down the road towards Bishop Auckland.

Arthur's lads set off after him, in all their motley glory. They formed a posse of galloping human dirt in shabby sweaters and mucky jeans. Luckily for them, a coach pulled alongside as they ran down the road. The driver offered them a lift and soon wished he hadn't. A strong, silent type, he said nothing until the stench became overpowering, then looking reproachfully at the company in general he said: 'By God, you buggers stink!'

The horse, triumphant but tired, was finally cornered. His stable-girl was in tears, as one of her colleagues heartlessly pointed out that there were doubtless pieces of him everywhere down the frantic route. But, by some miracle, Super Mikado was patched up to racing standard. The postscript is enough to bring a shiver down my jockey's spine.

In the filming of 'Champions', the screen version of the story chronicling Bob Champion's fight against cancer and his eventual Grand National success on Aldaniti, a good deal of extras – both horse and human – were needed to simulate the running of the National over the actual Aintree fences. A lot of jockeys were enlisted, and trainers were asked, at a price, to provide horses for the filming days. Trainers were well paid for the inconvenience and most co-operated but, inevitably, some of the offered horses were injured or sick when the scheduled filming times arrived and replacements were needed. Graham Bradley was among the riders involved and, having selected his own ride, he was circling around waiting for the cameras to roll, when he noticed Martin Pepper, another northern rider, hop on board a big, ugly animal he seemed to recognise. 'Brad', frustrated that he could not place the horse, asked the girl leading him up for his name. 'Super Mikado' was the reply. Now, the one thing you can say about jockeys is that they soon pick up information about thorough rogues. Martin Pepper needed half a second to dismount and scamper away in search of a more suitable ride. Super Mikado, friendless in the jockey market, eventually had to be withdrawn from the set.

The early hours demanded by the job dictate that many trainers are not at their cheeriest when supervising first lot on the gallops. Some, of course, are grouchier than others, and any who have crossed, shall we say, Fred Winter or David Nicholson soon after dawn on a winter morning, will know what it is to feel the sharp end of someone's tongue.

Tales about David are legion. Most of them are even true! Not for nothing is he commonly known as 'The Duke' and his amusingly overbearing attitudes on the cricket pitch have been a source of wicked anecdotes for many years. At home, in his yard and on his gallops, he leaves nobody in any doubt about who is in charge. Fair enough, too – it would be a brave man who disputed that David's is among the most efficiently run of all jumping yards, and his steady, annual success pays tributes to his methods. Occasionally, however, 'The Duke' can parody his own popular image.

Early one morning, out on the work-grounds at Condicote, 'The Duke' was astride his hack, addressing the 'troops' in his gruffest tones, when the string of horses was startled by a hot-air balloon fly-ing low over the field. David was predictably irate and, as if designed to infuriate him still further, the joy-rider in the balloon was leaning out of his rather ridiculous basket, grinning and waving wildly.

Uttering a few well-chosen oaths, 'The Duke' realised that he was at something of a height disadvantage in any ensuing exchange. Thinking quickly to counter this, he stood up in his irons. Then, jabbing his index finger in a way which will be familiar to all who have debated a point with this great racing character, he bellowed at the innocent bloke: 'Why don't you bugger off and find some work to do!'

David Nicholson's wife, Dinah, is a charming lady. She can also be formidable when roused. Certain aspects of the house and yard at Condicote are Dinah's domain, and David, being basically a wise man, does not interfere. 'Mother', as he calls her, would not be pleased.

One of Dinah's great pride and joys around the stable used to be (and may still be for all I know) the chickens. She fed them, bred them and generally gave them the run of the place. The lads, knowing this, would treat the birds with some respect . . . but then Roy Mangan was never one for the niceties of life.

Roy had been riding out one day when he noticed a smart car at the front of David's house. It belonged to Nigel Twiston-Davies, a local farmer and later the trainer of that splendid little mare, Mrs Muck. Nigel used to ride work for David and also ride a few in amateurs' races. A foul plot, if you will pardon the pun, was sprung in the lively mind of Mangan.

At the top of the yard, he cornered one of the prize chickens, picked it up and set off towards the gate. Spying 'The Duke', emerging from the conservatory building he uses as an office, he stuffed the chicken inside his jacket and hurried on. Nothing was said. Reaching the far side of the house, he opened the door of Nigel's car (racing folk too often tend to leave their cars unlocked, as I know to my cost!) and made the bird comfortable in the back seat, winding the window down a few inches as he left, to ensure a supply of air. Then he went about his duties and awaited developments.

There was, predictably, a stewards' enquiry in the Nicholsons' court-room at which a baffled Twiston-Davies (Mr) denied any bid to steal one of the lady Nicholson's pets. By a process of elimination, not difficult when you have a man like Mangan about the yard, the identity of the culprit was indicated. David was told by Dinah that it was his job to speak to him.

Next morning at first lot, Roy walked his horse onto the gallops, where 'The Duke' was already imperiously stationed on his hack. Summoned in the usual manner, Roy went across for the expected dressing-down. 'Now then,' David began, looking his sternest. 'That chicken . . . "Mother" was not best pleased, you know.' With that, he could keep it in no longer. 'The Duke' and Roy simultaneously burst out laughing.

In the same era as Roy Mangan, came Paul Carvill, another native of Condicote, another of 'The Duke's' regular jockeys who never quite hit the big time . . . and a man more accident-prone than any I have known in racing.

When he first joined David's yard as a fresh-faced and impressionable lad straight out of school, Paul was the subject of the usual sort of wind-up from the older and more senior lads. They told him that after first lot, it was his job to go up to the village shop, on horseback, and buy all the sweets and cakes anyone might want. On complaining that he might be caught, he was naturally told that 'The Duke' would be off racing by that time and there was no fear of it.

Because he had done very little riding, Paul had only been given a pony to canter around on, and it was aboard this animal that he made his way up the pretty Cotswold lane to the stores.

Inevitably, he was unlucky. David had been delayed in setting off for the day's meeting and, as he nosed his car up through the village, he was understandably surprised to see this pony tied up outside when, to the best of his knowledge, Carvill and the other lads were beavering away at the menial tasks of keeping the yard spick and span. At that very moment, Paul appeared, his arms piled high with sweets, cigarettes and cakes. Seeing 'The Duke' pulling up in his car, his eyes grew wide and his face covered over with fright. He panicked, tried to mount the pony while urging him onwards at the same time and ended up lying astride his back while the poor, startled animal set off up the road at a respectable speed. Paul eventually fell off, by which time he had left indelible evidence of his crimes in the shape of a winding trail of sweets and other goodies stretching a hundred yards up the road.

Now, 'The Duke' may sometimes like to appear a hard man, but underneath it all there lies a very kind heart. Knowing stable-lads as well as he does, he had an accurate idea of the con-trick which had been played on Paul. Later that day, at evening stables, I am told he called all the lads together and issued a group bollocking with only one exemption – the amazed and grateful Carvill.

A close inspection of Paul Carvill's hands will reveal that he is missing a sizeable chunk off the end of a finger. This should be explained.

Slightly later in his career as a jockey, he had just completed riding out at Condicote and was leading his horse back into his box. At the back of the box is what is known as a rat-chain, to which the horse can be tied. He was in the process of doing this when something frightened the horse and he reared violently, twisting away from the noise so sharply that Paul's hand was caught agonisingly in the chain, detaching this lump from his finger. This, however, is not the end of the story, merely the beginning.

Paul, white and pained, was driven to hospital by Mrs Nicholson. The doctor, having viewed the evidence, decided that the finger could still be stitched and asked for the missing end. This presented a problem as, in the bedlam which had followed the accident, nobody had located it. Dinah telephoned the yard where David, delegating skilfully, instructed John Suthern to go and hunt for it.

John, another on the Nicholson jockeys' team, managed to conquer his squeamishness sufficiently to find the finger and wrap it up in some tissue paper. Then he put it in his car and set off at high speed for the hospital, where the doctor was waiting to perform some intricate surgery.

It was only when he got there that he realised his great mistake. You see, John had a dog which travelled with him everywhere – even in emergencies like this. You can almost guess the rest. The dog, perhaps a little peckish as lunchtime approached, had investigated the tissue paper, found something which looked edible – and that was the end of Paul Carvill's finger!

In conclusion on this most unfortunate man, I am pleased to tell a story of a time when fortune did smile on him rather amusingly. To appreciate the significance in this, one has to know that Paul, a devout Catholic, is nicknamed 'Pope' and that the season in question is 1981–2, when the Pope himself was attracting vast crowds on his tour of the United Kingdom.

It was, I recall, a Bank Holiday weekend. Paul had no booked rides and was going through a very bleak time, but he had picked up a spare for the following day at Kelso, of all places, and he interrupted his drive to Scotland to drop in at Towcester and collect some of his gear from the valets.

He was immediately told that Robert Hughes had not arrived from his Epsom home and he could, if he wished, ride a hurdler called Gazaan in his place. He could and he wished. The horse won, and Robert Hughes arrived just as the connections were surrounding their winner. On being asked what had delayed him, he explained that he had been caught up in the traffic heading for the Pope's latest address! Perhaps there is something to divine intervention, after all.

Things can happen at morning exercise which seem hilarious to all except the person concerned. On a personal level, I think ruefully back to the January morning a couple of years ago when I was due to give the triple Champion Hurdler See You Then his first schooling session of the winter. Puffed up with pride, as anyone would be in getting aboard this wonderful animal, I found that the feeling was not mutual. No sooner had I swung my leg across him than he violently bucked me off again. I hung on to the reins, which eased the alarm in the eyes of Nick Henderson, but in glancing around the assembled work-riders from my undignified position in the Lambourn mud I could detect an embarrassing degree of merriment.

I imagine the same sense of public humiliation was rather exaggerated within a lad called Mick, who was attached to a northern trainer by the name of Tommy Robson in the late 1960s. Ian

Watkinson was also working for Robson at the time and he recalls that they used to work the horses round a copse, which could only be reached by way of an extremely narrow path, no more than a horse's width wide. They were walking up this path one morning when Mick, who was at the front of the string on a big horse called Sungod, loudly announced that he needed to relieve himself.

Taking the reins over the horse's head, he hopped off and went behind a bush, dropping his trousers and going about his essential business. The rest of the horses and riders stood waiting, the girls a shade embarrassed – though doubtless they had seen something like this before. They may not, however, have seen anything like what followed.

From behind the bush there suddenly came the unmistakable sound of a resounding fart. Sungod, taking exception to such rudery, decided he had been in close company with this man quite long enough and promptly bolted. The problem was that Mick still had hold of his reins and, being the faithful stable-lad he was, he did not let go. The result was a farcical sight: Sungod pulling a reluctant Mick out of the bush, his trousers and pants hanging limp around his ankles and nothing covering his embarrassment.

Phil Tuck is one of the very best jockeys in the north, Gordon Richards one of the most capable trainers. Together they make a formidable team. One of Phil's other talents, however, is as a mimic, and he delights in telling irreverent stories about people he has come across in racing, suitably embellished with splendid impressions of voice and action. Most are unprintable, but he does tell a lovely tale about Gordon which should cause no offence.

Trainers sometimes have a habit of addressing even the most senior riders like children. I have experienced it many times, and, on this particular morning on the gallops at the Richards HQ in Greystoke, Cumbria, Phil was getting the treatment from Gordon. The gist of it was that Gordon, having himself broken in a rather mulish three-year-old, believed that Phil was not giving the horse much assistance on the gallops. 'You have to get hold of him and make him work,' he complained.

Phil was then instructed to work the three-year-old over a six-furlong gallop, with another of the stable's decent horses. Gordon set off towards the end of the gallop while Phil had a quiet word with the rider of the second horse. 'Whatever happens,' he said, 'I'm finishing in front of you – do you understand?' The other lad, having been witness to Gordon's remarks, understood perfectly and the work went to plan, Phil nudging his horse past a hard-held opponent to finish half-a-length up.

Gordon came across and asked if he had felt alright this time. 'Of course he did,' replied Phil. "I got hold of him and made him work, just like you said!"

The combination of Mick Easterby, who can be the most forthright of northerners, and Ronnie Beggan, who can be the most perplexing of Irishmen, has endless possibilities. The first time they came across each other in a working environment illustrates my point.

Ronnie, who likes to put himself around and is never scared of phoning trainers to offer his services, had arranged to ride out on a fairly regular basis at Mick's yard in the village of Sherrif Hutton, just outside York. At the time, Ronnie was attached to the Dickinson yard at Harewood, further south in Yorkshire. It was not much of a journey but, predictably, Ronnie was late. In fact, he was very late.

On Ronnie's arrival Mick was standing in the centre of his yard and in no mood to pull punches. 'Where've you bloody been, Beggan?' he demanded. 'Ah, I'm sorry sir, I got myself lost in the one-way system in York sir,' spluttered Ronnie (and you must imagine the Irish brogue). 'What did you do – go back to bloody Harewood and start again?' said Mick, before dismissing the hapless Beggan from his attentions.

When stable-lads get together, out of earshot of their guv'nor, they moan. Of course they do – they are no different from the workforce in any other employer–employee situation. Just occasionally, though, the moaning might get a little too vitriolic, a little too malignant. Then the trainer has to act.

I'm told this happened recently in the yard of a Lambourn trainer who handles a few jumpers and rather more flat horses. He took action in the most unconventional way. One morning he left word that he would be delayed on the way to the gallops and the lads should ride the horses he had indicated on a worksheet and wait for him at an appointed place up on the working grounds. They followed orders, moaning as loudly as usual, and gathered on the gallops, circling their horses under a tree.

What they did not know was that their trainer had not been delayed at all. He was there ahead of them, comfortably seated in the aforesaid tree, camouflaged by some thick greenery.

He apparently let them fester for ten minutes or more, listened to all their assorted moans and groans and then (and I would love to have been witness to this) jumped down in the most theatrical manner and sacked the lot of them.

Stewards And Starters

Leaving aside the connections of the horses we ride, there are various individuals who can have a significant bearing on a jockey's day. The clerk of the scales presents a hurdle to be crossed several times each race-day, but I have dealt with him elsewhere. Once out on the racecourse, the starter is an important man, to be crossed at one's peril. If you have a particularly temperamental horse to ride, a decent break is usually essential, and you are very much in the hands of the gentleman on the rostrum. Upset him, and the rest of the field could easily be on their way without you.

Then, of course, there are the stewards, that band of dignified, well-bred men whose brief is to ensure the smooth and fair running of the meeting. Sometimes, they have to investigate matters entirely beyond the control of jockeys and trainers – the recent fiasco at

Chepstow, when a running rail was across the course during a novice chase, is one such example. But the great majority of their more publicised business concerns the riding of horses and the conduct of jockeys.

Sometimes, trainers are called in to explain why one of their horses has run either very much better or very much worse than its recent form would suggest to be likely. Occasionally, one particular trainer attracts such regular investigation by the stewards that it becomes obvious he has crossed the borderline in their minds and become plain suspicious. One such recent example is Barney Curley, an intrepid punter who grew tired of paying training bills so began to train some horses himself. He had enough trouble obtaining a licence; when he got one, and began to achieve a degree of success with a group of pretty modest horses, the stewards would not leave him alone. His method was plain enough – he had a number of horses who had broken down on the flat, patched them up enough to win a little race somewhere and placed them cleverly. This type of horse was never likely to run two races the same (dodgy legs would probably not allow it) but because Barney is a larger-than-life character who stood to win a great deal of money from certain well-publicised bets on the amount of winners he might train, the stewards considered it was their duty to keep him under constant scrutiny. Now, I don't pretend to know whether there was anything to substantiate their suspicions, or whether it was simply that some stewards regarded Mr Curley as an undesirable within their domain. For all their attentions, though, he survived to train the requisite number of winners and to claim his cash on the bet – and I think most people in racing, being of a breed which relishes personalities, were very pleased for him.

I would however be the first to concede that stewards have a difficult and sensitive job. If most of racing is a great deal purer than the more lurid public imaginations might believe, not everybody is involved for the good of the sport. Sorting the fiddlers from the fair-minded is something I would hate to have to do.

One of the biggest headaches of the stewards' job, and probably the most controversial aspect of racing as a whole is identifying the non-triers – the horses who have been dispatched by their trainers with no intention of winning. Punters often misunderstand motives when cases of this nature occur; they assume it means everyone connected with the horse is cheating and, in some way, gaining financially. Nothing could be farther from the truth; in almost every instance, the theory is to give a young horse some racecourse experience and discover if he will ever be any good, or to give a recently injured horse an 'easy' first race back. This does not alter the fact that it is against the specific rules of racing and that the stewards, if finding a case proven, have to take action. It does, however, lead to some very amusing situations . . .

There used to be a starter in the north of England called Colonel Smith. Typical of the times, he was a man out of the military who probably found work easy to come by in racing. By all accounts, he took a pretty casual attitude, his view apparently being that it was the jockeys' job to start the race properly, his being simply to let the tape go. If the field was in anything resembling a straight line, he would let them go, no matter that quite a few might be facing the wrong direction.

Safety limits, that very sensible innovation by which each course sets a maximum allowable number of runners for each type and distance of race, were still a thing of the future in Colonel Smith's day, and, one afternoon, he was confronted by no fewer than thirty-five runners for a novice hurdle at Catterick.

Watching them all mill around at the start, the Colonel mounted his rostrum and shouted: 'Now look here, I don't give a damn, but you might as well be safe so we'll do it this way – triers line up at the front, non-triers at the back!'

I have since heard this story repeated on a number of occasions, always with a different starter's name attached. If it has become part of racing's folklore, so be it . . . I still like to think it actually happened on a bleak day in north Yorkshire.

Jockeys can sometimes be embarrassed by a request, from a trainer or owner, to give a horse an 'easy' and finish no closer than fifth or sixth. On the one hand, the jockey will know he is strictly breaking the rules and risking disciplinary action; on the other, he will probably reason that he is doing nothing very serious and that if all goes well he will keep the ride for when the horse is 'off' and trying. It is a perennial dilemma which we have all faced at one time or another.

I am told that an old Australian trainer had a very appropriate maxim for such situations. He was not averse to instructing his jockey to finish out of the placings but, as he gave him a leg up into the saddle he would add: 'Listen, you know what's wanted – but if you hit the straight going too well, mate, just remind yourself: "Better three cheers than three years".'

The stewards' view of a race and the respective merits of the runners and riders will not always, thank heavens, coincide with that of the punters who have lost their money. Sometimes the furious punter will swallow his indignation, usually he will give vent to his grievances in the bars, where it can do very little harm. Just occasionally, however, a wounded gambler has a rather wider medium.

There is a famous story in Australia about a racecourse commentator who had backed a beaten favourite, and backed him heavily. Unlike in England, the course commentaries in Australia are also transmitted live by local radio stations, which means the man behind the microphones has two audiences – and two switches in front of him, one controlling the circuit to the course loudspeakers, the other his link with radio outlets.

Both switches are normally flicked to 'off' as soon as the runners are past the post, but the hole in his pocket had plainly taken its toll of this commentator's efficiency. Completing his reading of the race, he turned angrily to his mate in the box and snarled: 'Jesus, I don't mind backing a loser, but I sure like to back a trier now and again. That crooked bastard of a jockey was pulling his back teeth out.'

I cannot believe it was long before someone rushed in to tell the hapless man that his outburst had been heard all over the course, not to mention by the thousands tuned in to their radio sets. I don't know if the guy is still working as a commentator, but I'm told the tape of his *faux pas* is still circulating in New South Wales!

* * *

My old riding sidekick Ian Watkinson tells me he went to school in Suffolk with the son of a well-known Newmarket trainer, who for these purposes had better remain nameless. Ian and his friend obviously shared a common passion for racing and spent most of their time talking about runners and riders, rather than reading and writing. One day, the other boy rushed into the school and told Ian that his father had laid out a horse specifically for an apprentice race at Newmarket. The appointed jockey, a very raw if promising teenager, had dutifully given the animal two 'easies' in preparation and everyone was now satisfied that the day had come on which they could have a touch.

Apparently, however, the young jockey's excitement rather got the better of him. Some while before going out to ride, he was flapping agitatedly around the scales area. A stipendiary steward, more irritated than suspicious, impatiently wondered if the boy had been on the trial scales (where you can test your weight away from the eagle eye of the clerk of the scales). 'Have you tried yet?' the 'stipe' asked innocently. 'Not yet sir, but we're trying today!'

Sometimes, the stewards have to rule on very curious or obscure objections – maybe never more frequently than in Ireland. There was a meeting at Wexford in 1987 when a jockey named Pat O'Donnell was riding a fancied horse in a ten-runner steeplechase. Pat finished last of the ten but immediately lodged an objection to all nine in front of him for taking the wrong course. The stewards were obliged to go through the motions of an inquiry but, on studying their video patrol film they discovered that the first nine home had, indeed, raced the wrong side of a marker at the turn into the straight. The objection was sustained, nine horses were disqualified and last-placed Pat was promoted to first.

The most galling way for a jockey to lose a race is in the stewards' room and, although thankfully it has not yet happened to me, I can think of no more frustrating reason for disqualification than failing to weigh in.

Officially, every rider of a placed horse (and, after random races, every single rider) must sit on the scales before making any move to return to the changing-room. If you so much as pass the scales without weighing in you may be the subject of an objection from the clerk of the scales or, on certain occasions, from another jockey. I know of at least a couple of occasions in recent years when the rider of a runner-up has profitted from the absent-mindedness of the winner and come out of it with the race.

John Jenkins, now a successful trainer for whom I regularly ride, tells a story of his days as a struggling jockey. He was at Uttoxeter and had managed to galvanise some mediocre horse into giving enough of his best to finish in the frame. Back in the unsaddling enclosure, the horse's owner held court at enormous length (as some owners are wont to do in moments of minor, unexpected triumph). By the end of the monologue, John was thoroughly confused over whether he had done exceptionally well or downright badly, but was so pleased to escape that he scuttled up the steps and turned left straight into the weighing-room. He realised, even as he went through the door, that he had forgotten to weigh in and knew that discovery would bring inevitable disqualification and, worst of all, another more acrimonious lecture from the voluble owner.

Thinking remarkably swiftly, he kept walking, still carrying his saddle and tack, went to the back of the weighing-room, climbed rapidly out of a convenient window, walked back around to the front of the building and entered again, sitting quietly on the scales as if nothing had happened. Now that is what I call presence of mind!

Australian racing seems to breed more than its fair share of characters. Another I have been told of is the trainer who had an outstandingly quick sprinter in his yard. This horse would have run up a sequence of wins in five-furlong races, but for being terribly slow out of the starting-stalls. Time after time, the animal was left flat-footed – and, if you have been left at the start of a five-furlong dash, there is no way back.

The trainer was desperate for a coup. He was very short of money and he knew this horse represented his only chance to get out of

110

trouble. So, when next he appeared on a racecourse, at a course called Kensington, the trainer devised a cunning plan.

He deputed his foreman (he would be called the head lad in Britain) to saddle the horse, talk to the owners and give the jockey a leg-up. Then, having ensured that substantial wagers had been placed at rewarding odds, he went down to the five-furlong start, which was conveniently just in front of a small copse. It was the work of a moment to secrete himself in the bushes behind the stalls before the runners came down; the crucial part of the plan, however, required split-second timing.

He waited impatiently, doubtless nervously, while the girths of the runners were checked and the horses were loaded into the stalls. Then he watched the starter go across to his position. Just as the lever was pulled and the starter was yelling 'Go', the trainer dashed out from the scrub and, with pinpoint accuracy, cracked a long stockwhip on the rump of his horse, who duly scorched out of the stalls like a startled rabbit, led from start to finish and won easily.

The stewards, apprised by the starter of this eccentric occurrence, held the inevitable inquiry, called the trainer before them and fined him, adding a warning about his future conduct. The fine, however, was for a relatively negligible amount – his winnings were certainly not.

When the major handicap races come around each jumping season, there is invariably a good deal of moaning among trainers about the practice of declaring a high-class horse at the four-day stage, with no intention of running, simply to compress the weights at the lower end of the handicap. Occasionally, this practice goes even further and the topweight is left in overnight so that the weights do not rise at all (usually to the benefit of another horse in the same stable). Stewards rightly inquire into obvious instances and recently some big-name trainers have been brought to book on the issue.

Lambourn was aflame with indignation when Rod Simpson, one of racing's more colourful characters, declared two horses for a big handicap at Sandown Park a few seasons ago. His fancied runner was nicely weighted, well down the handicap, but the horse keeping the weights down was also his. Many other trainers, whose horses were condemned to carrying more weight than they had been allotted by this tactic, openly predicted that Rod's top-weighted horse would be withdrawn a few hours before the race. Whether simply to spite the rumour-mongers or because he always intended to, I can't say, but Rod decided to run both his horses. A young apprentice was given the ride on the topweight and Rod's instructions were to drop him out early in the race, then get him involved in the straight if he was capable.

The horse declined to involve himself at all and was pulled up. The stewards, who had naturally been monitoring the saga from its outset, called trainer and jockey into an inquiry and asked the boy to repeat the instructions he had been given. This he managed to do, fairly faithfully, though with a good deal of nervous stammering. Rod was apparently finding the whole thing amusing, as he would, but after a while he noticed that the jockey was hopping agitatedly from one foot to the other. Looking behind him, he could see he was standing directly in front of a three-bar electric fire which was burning the backs of his legs.

Rod immediately interrupted the flow of one of the stewards and, to their surprise, turned to the lad and said: 'Listen, even in here they won't burn you at the stake, so don't act like Joan of Arc.'